the big book of more baking with refrigerated dough

Houghton Mifflin Harcourt

Boston • New York

www.hmhco.com

Library of Congress Cataloging-in-Publication Data is available.

ISBN 978-0-544-64870-8 (trade paper)
ISBN 978-0-544-72730-4 (ebk.)

GENERAL MILLS

Owned Media and Publishing Director: Amy Halford

Owned Media and Publishing Manager: Audra Carson

Senior Editor: Grace Wells

Food Editors: Lori Fox, Mary Kaye Sahli, and Cathy Swanson

Recipe Development and Testing: Betty Crocker Kitchens

Photography: General Mills Photography Studios and Image Library

HOUGHTON MIFFLIN HARCOURT

Publisher: Natalie Chapman

Editorial Director: Cindy Kitchel

Executive Editor: Anne Ficklen

Editorial Associate: Molly Aronica

Managing Editor: Marina Padakis

Associate Production Editor: Helen Seachrist

Cover Design: Tai Blanche

Interior Design and Layout: Tai Blanche

Senior Production Coordinator: Kimberly Kiefer

Manufactured in China

SCP 10 9 8 7 6 5 4 3 2

4500649805

Cover Photos: Spicy Sausage and Kimchi Pizza (page 130), Baked Banana-Cookie Doughnuts (page 256), Creamy Corn-Filled Sweet Peppers (page 42), Pickled n' Twisted Spicy Pork Cemitas (page 96), Chocolate-Raspberry Crescent Ring (page 276) Loaded Baked Potato Pizza (page 139), Biscuit Pepperoni Pizza Bake (page 186), Mango Tango Teriyaki Sliders (page 105), Strawberry-Rhubarb Mini Pies (page 240)

Home of the Pillsbury Bake-Off® Contest

Pillsbury

For more great recipes visit
pillsbury.com

Dear Friends,

Our book, *The Big Book of Easy Baking with Refrigerated Dough*, was such a hit we knew we had to create a sequel with new ideas and beautiful photographs. Once again the pages are filled with no-fuss recipes all starting with the convenience of refrigerated dough products. *The Big Book of More Baking with Refrigerated Dough* is here for the entire family to enjoy.

Every recipe in this tasty collection uses one of our time-saving products to create a little refrigerated dough magic. You'll find appetizers, sandwiches, pizzas, casseroles and a variety of sweet treats to try. Plus, there are gluten-free recipes in here too.

Be sure to check out our features on baked doughnuts and grilled pizzas. All the great tastes of the doughnut shop or pizza restaurant are made simple with easy-to-use refrigerated dough. Many recipes from the famous Bake-Off® Contest appear too, and these recipes are always fun to make. Try Loaded Potato Pinwheels, page 32, Peppered Bacon–Wrapped Turkey Pub Sandwiches, page 72, or Ooey-Gooey Turtle Bars, page 314.

Go for the dough, then shape it, wrap it, fill it, stuff it or top it into something delicious everyone will love. Let the baking begin!

Our Best to You,

The Pillsbury Editors

P.S. Look for these helpful icons throughout the book:

6-INGREDIENTS OR LESS

QUICK For recipes that take 30 minutes or less start to finish

contents

make and bake it easy with pillsbury refrigerated dough

During the 1950s, modern conveniences were on the rise in America, including the introduction of innovative refrigerated dough products that could be found at the grocery store. These products were quick to become favorites in homes across the country, with satisfied consumers enjoying the versatility, aroma and taste of freshly baked dough.

Over the years, Pillsbury dough products have continued to provide ease of preparation and delicious results. It's easy to just pop the can, make and bake—but what is more fun is the array of recipes available using those great products. Plus, the times have helped dictate new products, from different crescent roll creations and artisan pizza crust to gluten-free dough, plus inspired new food ideas to match.

Although we love the convenience of refrigerated dough, some tips will help you to get the best results when you use refrigerated dough products.

- Store dough on a shelf in the refrigerator. Temperatures on the door or in the crisper may be too warm or too cool.
- Keep dough refrigerated in the package or can until just before you use it. After you open the package, use the product right away or the dough may become sticky or hard to handle.
- Do not freeze dough products because the leavening will be inactivated and the dough will not rise. Exceptions to this are pie crust and cookie dough. Packages will indicate if freezing is possible and for how long.
- Always use dough by the expiration date on the end of the can or on the package. Exceptions to this are pie crust and cookie dough, both of which can be frozen up to 2 months.
- For the dough to bake correctly, always preheat the oven before baking.
- Serve refrigerated dough products warm from the oven unless the recipe specifies something different.
- Dough products should not be cooked in the microwave oven.

Tips for Baking Gluten Free

Feeling left out because you are eating gluten-free is a thing of the past because our gluten-free refrigerated dough products let you make cookies, pies and even pizza. For the best results, make sure to follow the directions on the package and in individual recipes. Here are some basic go-to baking tips to help make your gluten-free baking adventures a success.

- The best way to know if a product is gluten free is to read the ingredient listing on the label.
- Cell phones are a handy tool while shopping in case you need to call the 800 number on a product to verify whether or not it is truly gluten free.
- Keep a wide variety of gluten-free ingredients on hand for convenience.
- Store Pillsbury gluten-free dough products on a shelf in the refrigerator and keep them cold until just before using.
- For the best results with Pillsbury dough products, use by the expiration date on the package.
- When making gluten-free foods, it's important to keep things free from contact with gluten. Keep the kitchen and all equipment that is used for gluten-free cooking very clean to help eliminate this problem. It's good to keep separate cutting boards and a separate area for food preparation if possible.
- Gluten-free baked goods tend to dry out more quickly than those made with wheat, so follow recipe storage directions.
- Create "gluten-safe" kitchen practices by designating one or more shelves just for these items, and consider using the upper shelves so gluten-containing food particles don't fall down on the shelves. Place ingredients in sealed containers and use color-coding or label them.

CHAPTER 1

appetizers

cauliflower breadsticks

prep time: 20 Minutes • **start to finish:** 1 Hour 25 Minutes • 24 breadsticks

- 4 cups fresh cauliflower florets (from 1 small head)
- 2 tablespoons olive oil
- 1 can Pillsbury refrigerated Crescent Dough Sheet
- 1¼ cups shredded pepper Jack cheese (5 oz)
- 1 egg white
- ⅛ teaspoon salt
- 1 tablespoon chopped fresh cilantro

1 Heat oven to 375°F. In large bowl, toss cauliflower and oil; spread in single layer in ungreased 15x10x1-inch pan. Bake 25 to 30 minutes, turning once, until tender and golden brown. Cool 5 minutes.

2 Place cauliflower in food processor. Cover; process 2 to 3 minutes, scraping side once with rubber spatula, until cauliflower looks like fine crumbs. Set aside.

3 Unroll dough on large ungreased cookie sheet; starting at center, press dough into 10x8-inch rectangle. Bake 8 to 12 minutes or until golden brown.

4 Meanwhile, in medium bowl, stir together cauliflower, cheese, egg white and salt until well blended. Spread mixture over partially baked dough.

5 Bake 10 to 15 minutes or until edges are deep golden brown and cheese is melted. Sprinkle with cilantro. Using pizza cutter or knife, cut in half lengthwise, then cut crosswise into 12 rows. Serve warm.

1 Breadstick: Calories 70; Total Fat 4g (Saturated Fat 1.5g, Trans Fat 0g); Cholesterol 5mg; Sodium 130mg; Total Carbohydrate 5g (Dietary Fiber 0g); Protein 2g **Exchanges:** ½ Starch, ½ Fat **Carbohydrate Choices:** ½

Easy Success Tip

For a less spicy flavor, substitute sharp Cheddar cheese for the pepper Jack.

toasted tuscan walnut squares

prep time: 20 Minutes • **start to finish:** 50 Minutes • 24 appetizers

- ½ cup coarsely chopped walnuts
- 1 can Pillsbury refrigerated classic pizza crust
- ⅔ cup basil pesto
- 1 box (9 oz) frozen chopped spinach, thawed, squeezed to drain
- ½ cup sun-dried tomatoes in oil, patted dry, cut into ¼-inch slices
- ½ cup well-drained artichoke hearts (from 14-oz can), coarsely chopped
- 1 cup crumbled feta cheese (4 oz)
- 1 cup shredded mozzarella cheese (4 oz)

1 Heat oven to 350°F. Spread walnuts in ungreased shallow pan. Bake 6 to 10 minutes, stirring occasionally, until light brown. Set aside.

2 Increase oven temperature to 400°F for dark or nonstick pan (425°F for all other pans). Lightly spray large cookie sheet or 15x10x1-inch pan with cooking spray. Unroll dough on cookie sheet; starting at center, press dough into 15x10-inch rectangle. Bake 8 to 12 minutes or until edges are light golden brown.

3 Spread pesto over partially baked crust. Top evenly with spinach, tomatoes, artichoke hearts and cheeses.

4 Bake 8 to 15 minutes or until crust is golden brown and cheese is melted. Sprinkle with walnuts. Cut into 6 rows by 4 rows. Serve warm.

1 Appetizer: Calories 130; Total Fat 8g (Saturated Fat 2.5g; Trans Fat 0g); Cholesterol 10mg; Sodium 270mg; Total Carbohydrate 10g (Dietary Fiber 0g); Protein 5g **Exchanges:** ½ Starch, ½ Medium-Fat Meat, 1 Fat **Carbohydrate Choices:** ½

Easy Success Tip

Substitute toasted pine nuts for the walnuts and fontina or Italian cheese blend for the mozzarella.

green chile–cheese appetizers

prep time: 30 Minutes • **start to finish:** 55 Minutes • 24 appetizers

- 1 cup crumbled feta cheese (4 oz)
- 4 oz (half of 8-oz package) cream cheese, softened
- 3 tablespoons chopped green chiles (from 4.5-oz can)
- 1 egg, separated
- 1 tablespoon water
- 1 box Pillsbury refrigerated pie crusts, softened as directed on box
- 1 teaspoon sesame seed

1 Heat oven to 375°F. Line large cookie sheets with cooking parchment paper.

2 In small bowl, mix feta cheese, cream cheese, chiles and egg yolk until well blended; set aside. In another small bowl, beat egg white and water until blended; set aside.

3 Unroll pie crusts on work surface. Using 3-inch round cutter, cut 9 rounds from each crust. Gather scraps and reroll; cut 6 additional rounds.

4 Spoon slightly less than 1 tablespoon cheese mixture onto half of each dough round. Brush edges of rounds with egg white mixture. Fold rounds in half; press edges with fork to seal. Place on cookie sheet. Brush tops with egg white mixture; sprinkle with sesame seed.

5 Bake 18 to 25 minutes or until light golden brown. Serve warm.

1 Appetizer: Calories 110; Total Fat 7g (Saturated Fat 3.5g; Trans Fat 0g); Cholesterol 20mg; Sodium 180mg; Total Carbohydrate 9g (Dietary Fiber 0g); Protein 2g **Exchanges:** ½ Starch, 1½ Fat **Carbohydrate Choices:** ½

Easy Success Tip

Cold eggs right from the refrigerator are the easiest to separate.

Bake-Off® Contest 47, 2014 | **Marie Valdes** | Brandon, FL

spinach dip–stuffed garlic rolls

prep time: 30 Minutes • **start to finish:** 1 Hour • 12 appetizers

- ½ cup butter, melted
- 1 tablespoon garlic powder
- ⅔ cup grated Parmesan cheese
- 1 box (9 oz) frozen chopped spinach, thawed, squeezed to drain
- 4 oz (half of 8-oz package) cream cheese, softened
- 1 tablespoon Worcestershire sauce
- 1 can Pillsbury refrigerated crusty French loaf

1 Heat oven to 350°F. Spray 12 regular-size muffin cups with cooking spray. Spoon 1 teaspoon of the melted butter into each cup. Sprinkle ⅛ teaspoon of the garlic powder and 1 teaspoon of the Parmesan cheese into each cup.

2 In small bowl, mix spinach, cream cheese, 1 teaspoon of the garlic powder, ⅓ cup of the Parmesan cheese and the Worcestershire sauce until blended. Shape mixture into 12 (1½-inch) balls.

3 Cut dough into 12 equal slices. Press each slice into 3-inch round; place 1 spinach ball in center of each round. Carefully wrap dough around ball; pinch edges to seal completely. Place balls, seam side down, in muffin cups.

4 Bake 17 to 25 minutes or until golden brown. Cool 2 minutes. Loosen rolls with tip of knife. Remove from pan to serving plate. Brush rolls with remaining melted butter; sprinkle with remaining garlic powder and Parmesan cheese. Serve warm.

1 Appetizer: Calories 200; Total Fat 13g (Saturated Fat 8g; Trans Fat 0g); Cholesterol 35mg; Sodium 370mg; Total Carbohydrate 14g (Dietary Fiber 0g); Protein 5g **Exchanges:** 1 Starch, 2½ Fat **Carbohydrate Choices:** 1

Easy Success Tip

Substitute milk for the Worcestershire sauce if it's not your favorite flavor.

creamy smoked salmon cups

prep time: 30 Minutes • **start to finish:** 50 Minutes • 48 appetizers

- 4 oz (from 8-oz package) cream cheese, softened
- ½ cup sour cream
- 1 teaspoon lemon-pepper seasoning
- 2 tablespoons chopped fresh chives
- 2 teaspoons small capers, drained
- ¼ teaspoon salt
- 1 box (10 oz) frozen corn and butter sauce, thawed
- 4 oz smoked salmon, flaked
- 2 cans Pillsbury refrigerated crescent dinner rolls (8 rolls each) or 2 cans Pillsbury refrigerated Crescent Dough Sheet

1 Heat oven to 375°F. Spray 48 mini muffin cups with cooking spray.

2 In medium bowl, mix cream cheese and sour cream until well blended. Stir in lemon-pepper seasoning, chives, capers and salt. Stir in corn until well mixed. Fold in salmon.

3 If using crescent rolls: Unroll both cans of dough; separate into total of 8 rectangles. Firmly press perforations to seal. If using dough sheets: Unroll both cans of dough; cut into total of 8 rectangles.

4 Cut each rectangle into 6 (2-inch) squares. Press 1 square in bottom and up side of each muffin cup. Spoon slightly less than 1 tablespoon salmon filling into each cup.

5 Bake 10 to 18 minutes or until light golden brown. Cool 2 minutes; remove from pans to serving plate. Serve warm.

1 Appetizer: Calories 60; Total Fat 3.5g (Saturated Fat 1.5g; Trans Fat 0.5g); Cholesterol 0mg; Sodium 140mg; Total Carbohydrate 5g (Dietary Fiber 0g); Protein 1g **Exchanges:** ½ Starch, ½ Fat **Carbohydrate Choices:** ½

Bake-Off® Contest 47, 2014 | **Gary Smith** | Santa Rosa, CA

mini mexican gorditas

prep time: 35 Minutes • **start to finish:** 35 Minutes • 24 appetizers

- 1 box (10 oz) frozen corn and butter sauce
- 6 oz bulk chorizo sausage, crumbled
- 1 can Pillsbury Grands!™ Flaky Layers Original refrigerated biscuits (8 biscuits)
- 2 tablespoons vegetable oil
- 1 cup shredded pepper Jack cheese (4 oz)
- 1 avocado, pitted, peeled and cut into ½-inch cubes
- 2 teaspoons grated lemon peel
- 4½ teaspoons lemon juice
- ⅛ teaspoon kosher (coarse) salt
- ⅛ teaspoon pepper

1 Heat oven to 300°F. Microwave corn as directed on box.

2 Meanwhile, in 10-inch nonstick skillet, cook sausage over medium heat, stirring frequently, until thoroughly cooked. Drain on paper towels. Wipe skillet clean. In medium bowl, mix sausage and corn; set aside.

3 Separate dough into 8 biscuits; cut each biscuit into 3 wedges. Press or roll each wedge to form 3-inch round.

4 In same skillet, heat 1½ teaspoons of the oil over medium heat. Add 6 biscuit rounds; cook 2 to 4 minutes, turning once, until golden brown and cooked through. Place on ungreased cookie sheet; keep warm in oven. Repeat with remaining biscuit rounds, adding 1½ teaspoons oil to skillet for each batch.

5 Top each biscuit round with 1 tablespoon sausage-corn mixture and 2 teaspoons cheese. Bake 4 to 5 minutes or until hot and cheese is melted.

6 Meanwhile, in small bowl, mix avocado, lemon peel, lemon juice, salt and pepper. Spoon mixture evenly onto baked rounds. Serve warm.

1 Appetizer: Calories 130; Total Fat 8g (Saturated Fat 3g; Trans Fat 0g); Cholesterol 10mg; Sodium 310mg; Total Carbohydrate 11g (Dietary Fiber 0g); Protein 4g **Exchanges:** ½ Other Carbohydrate, ½ High-Fat Meat, 1 Fat **Carbohydrate Choices:** 1

Bake-Off® Contest 46, 2013 | **Gary Chiu** | Irving, TX

chinese pancakes with ponzu marmalade sauce

prep time: 30 Minutes • **start to finish:** 30 Minutes • 10 servings

- ⅓ cup ponzu citrus soy sauce
- ¼ cup low-sugar sweet orange marmalade
- 1 teaspoon chili garlic paste
- 2 teaspoons sesame seed, toasted*
- 2 tablespoons water
- 1 can Pillsbury Grands! Jr. Golden Layers™ Butter Tastin'™ refrigerated biscuits (10 biscuits)
- ⅓ cup finely chopped green onions (5 medium)
- Pepper to taste
- 2 tablespoons olive oil

1 In small bowl, mix soy sauce, marmalade, chili garlic paste, sesame seed and water; set aside.

2 Separate dough into 10 biscuits; cut each biscuit into 2 layers. Press each biscuit half into 4-inch round. Sprinkle 2 teaspoons onion on each of 10 biscuit rounds; sprinkle lightly with pepper. Top with remaining biscuit rounds; press and reshape into 4-inch rounds.

3 On nonstick griddle pan or in 12-inch nonstick skillet, heat oil over medium heat. Cook 3 to 4 filled biscuits at a time 2 to 4 minutes, turning once, until golden brown and no longer doughy. Drain on paper towels; cover to keep warm. Repeat with remaining biscuits, adding additional oil if necessary.

4 Cut pancakes into wedges. Serve warm with reserved sauce.

*To toast sesame seed, sprinkle in ungreased skillet. Cook over medium-low heat 5 to 7 minutes, stirring frequently until browning begins, then stirring constantly until golden brown.

1 Serving: Calories 150; Total Fat 7g (Saturated Fat 2g; Trans Fat 0g); Cholesterol 0mg; Sodium 590mg; Total Carbohydrate 20g (Dietary Fiber 1g); Protein 2g **Exchanges:** ½ Starch, 1 Other Carbohydrate, 1½ Fat **Carbohydrate Choices:** 1

gluten-free herbs-and-seeds parmesan crackers

prep time: 30 Minutes • **start to finish:** 45 Minutes • 18 crackers

- 1 container Pillsbury Gluten Free refrigerated pie and pastry dough
- ½ cup gluten-free grated Parmesan cheese
- 2 tablespoons poppy seed
- 2 tablespoons sesame seed
- 1 teaspoon dried rosemary leaves, crushed
- 1 teaspoon dried thyme leaves
- ½ teaspoon garlic powder

Easy Success Tip

If you are cooking gluten free, always read labels to make sure each recipe ingredient is gluten free. Products and ingredient sources can change.

1 Heat oven to 400°F. Cut 5 sheets cooking parchment paper the size of large cookie sheet. Place cookie sheet in oven to heat.

2 Place 1 parchment sheet on work surface; break up dough on sheet. Sprinkle 6 tablespoons of the Parmesan cheese, 1 tablespoon of the poppy seed, the sesame seed, rosemary, thyme and garlic powder over dough; knead with hands until softened, no longer crumbly and well mixed.

3 Shape dough into 18 (1½-inch) balls. Place 6 balls on second parchment sheet; top with another parchment sheet. With rolling pin, roll balls into 5x2½-inch ovals about 1/16 inch thick. Repeat with remaining balls, placing 6 balls on each sheet of parchment. Sprinkle crackers with remaining 1 tablespoon poppy seed. Prick each cracker several times with fork.

4 Remove cookie sheet from oven; carefully slide 1 parchment sheet with crackers onto hot cookie sheet. Bake 4 to 5 minutes or until edges are deep golden brown. Carefully slide parchment and crackers from cookie sheet to cooling rack. Sprinkle each cracker with about ¼ teaspoon of the remaining Parmesan cheese. Repeat with remaining crackers. Serve warm or cool. If desired, break crackers into smaller pieces to serve. Store in tightly covered container.

1 Cracker: Calories 140; Total Fat 9g (Saturated Fat 3.5g; Trans Fat 0g); Cholesterol 0mg; Sodium 200mg; Total Carbohydrate 11g (Dietary Fiber 0g); Protein 1g **Exchanges:** ½ Starch, 2 Fat **Carbohydrate Choices:** 1

Bake-Off® Contest 47, 2014 | **Amy Siegel** | Clifton, NJ

sesame mini pitas with roasted red pepper tapenade

prep time: 30 Minutes • **start to finish:** 30 Minutes • 16 servings

- ¼ cup sesame seed
- 1 container Pillsbury Gluten Free refrigerated pizza crust dough
- 1 tablespoon olive oil
- ½ cup drained pimiento-stuffed green olives
- 1 cup coarsely chopped drained roasted red bell peppers (from a jar)
- 3 tablespoons dried cilantro leaves
- 1 teaspoon garlic powder
- ¼ teaspoon fine sea salt
- ¼ teaspoon freshly ground pepper
- ¼ cup olive oil

1 Heat oven to 400°F. Line large cookie sheets with cooking parchment paper.

2 Place sesame seed in small bowl. Divide dough into 16 equal parts; shape each part into 1¼-inch ball. Coat balls with sesame seed, gently pressing seed into dough. On cookie sheets, place balls 3 inches apart. Place sheet of parchment paper on top of dough balls. Press flat-bottom drinking glass on each ball to form 3-inch round; remove parchment paper. Brush rounds with 1 tablespoon oil. Bake 6 to 9 minutes or until light golden brown. Cool 5 minutes.

3 Meanwhile, in food processor or blender, place olives, roasted peppers, cilantro, garlic powder, salt and pepper. Cover; process about 30 seconds, scraping sides occasionally, until finely chopped. Add ¼ cup oil. Cover; process with quick on-and-off motions until blended.

4 Spoon tapenade into serving bowl. Serve with warm mini pitas.

1 Serving: Calories 130; Total Fat 8g (Saturated Fat 1g; Trans Fat 0g); Cholesterol 0mg; Sodium 400mg; Total Carbohydrate 13g (Dietary Fiber 1g); Protein 1g **Exchanges:** 1 Starch, 1½ Fat **Carbohydrate Choices:** 1

Easy Success Tips

Tapenade can be made up to 3 days in advance; store covered in refrigerator. To reheat mini pitas, place on ungreased cookie sheet and bake at 350°F for 5 minutes.

If cooking gluten free, always read labels to make sure each recipe ingredient is gluten free. Products and ingredient sources can change.

turkey blt pinwheels

prep time: 20 Minutes • **start to finish:** 40 Minutes • 24 appetizers

- 1 can Pillsbury refrigerated Crescent Dough Sheet
- ¼ cup sun-dried tomato pesto (from 8.5-oz jar)
- 6 thin slices (1 oz each) cooked turkey breast (from deli)
- 1 cup lightly packed fresh baby kale mix or baby spinach leaves
- ¼ cup shredded Monterey Jack cheese (1 oz)
- 3 slices crumbled crisply cooked bacon (¼ cup)

1 Heat oven to 375°F. Spray large cookie sheet with cooking spray.

2 Unroll dough sheet on work surface or cutting board; starting at center, press dough into 12x9-inch rectangle. Spread pesto over rectangle to within ¼ inch of edges. Arrange turkey and kale over pesto; sprinkle with cheese and bacon.

3 Starting with long side, roll up rectangle; pinch seam to seal. With serrated knife, cut into 24 (½-inch) slices. Place slices, cut side down, on cookie sheet.

4 Bake 13 to 18 minutes or until golden brown. Immediately remove from cookie sheet to serving plate. Serve warm.

1 Appetizer: Calories 60; Total Fat 3.5g (Saturated Fat 1g, Trans Fat 0g); Cholesterol 5mg; Sodium 200mg; Total Carbohydrate 5g (Dietary Fiber 0g); Protein 3g **Exchanges:** ½ Starch, ½ Fat **Carbohydrate Choices:** ½

Easy Success Tip

Baby kale leaves are small (about the size of baby spinach leaves), tender and mild in flavor. Baby kale is sold as a single green but is often mixed with baby spinach.

Pinwheel Pizzazz

It's party time! And you're on a roll when you use Pillsbury refrigerated dough to create tasty, colorful pinwheel appetizers. Preparation is simple and deciding what to fill the pinwheels with is the fun part.

To make the pinwheels, use one can of refrigerated crescent dinner roll dough. Heat the oven to 375°F and lightly spray a cookie sheet with cooking spray. Unroll the crescent roll dough onto a work surface and separate into 2 long rectangles; press the perforations to seal. Top with desired ingredients (see below) to within ½ inch of edges. Starting with long side of each rectangle, roll up tightly. With a serrated knife, cut each roll into 8 slices and place on the cookie sheet. Bake 14 to 18 minutes or until light golden brown. Arrange the pretty pinwheel spirals on a decorative platter and serve warm—yum!

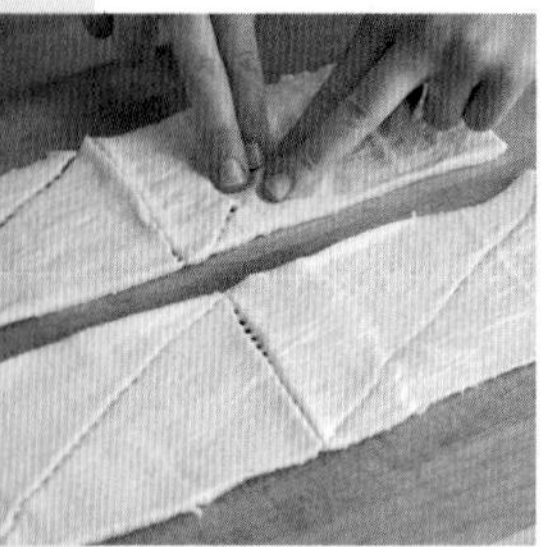

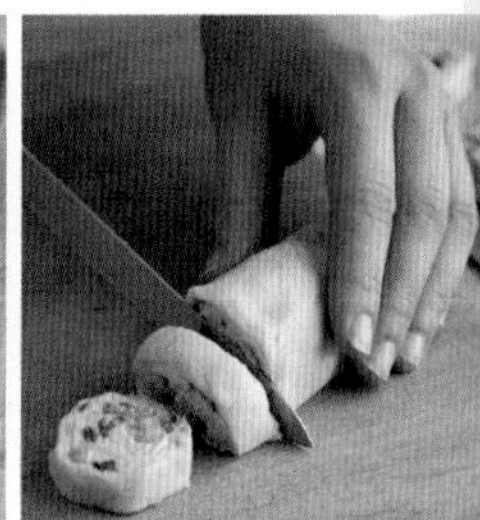

Use these filling combinations as a starting point, then use your imagination to create more fun ideas.

- **Bacon-Cheddar Pinwheels:** Spread dough with 2 tablespoons ranch dressing, 4 slices chopped cooked bacon, ½ cup finely shredded Cheddar cheese and 2 tablespoons chopped green onion. Roll and bake as directed.
- **Chicken and Swiss Pinwheels:** Spread dough with 2 tablespoons mustard-mayonnaise sauce. Sprinkle with ½ cup chopped cooked chicken, ½ cup shredded Swiss cheese and 2 tablespoons finely chopped green onion. Roll and bake as directed above.
- **Chile-Cheese Pinwheels:** Sprinkle dough with 2 tablespoons drained chopped green chiles, ¾ cup shredded Monterey Jack cheese and ½ cup chopped red bell pepper. Roll and bake as directed.
- **Pesto Turkey Pinwheels:** Spread dough with 2 tablespoons refrigerated pesto. Sprinkle with ½ cup chopped cooked turkey and 1 cup shredded mozzarella cheese. Roll and bake as directed.
- **Roast Beef Pinwheels:** Spread dough with 2 tablespoons spicy brown mustard. Layer with 6 thin slices deli roast beef, ½ cup chopped roasted bell peppers and 1 cup shredded lettuce. Roll and bake as directed.
- **Triple-Cheese Pinwheels:** Sprinkle dough with ½ cup each shredded Cheddar and shredded mozzarella and ¼ cup crumbled blue cheese. Drizzle with a few drops hot pepper sauce. Roll and bake as directed above.

jalapeño-chicken crescent pinwheels

prep time: 20 Minutes • **start to finish:** 40 Minutes • 32 appetizers

- 4 oz (half of 8-oz package) cream cheese, softened
- ½ cup chopped cooked chicken
- ¼ cup chopped fresh cilantro
- 2 to 3 tablespoons finely chopped pickled sliced jalapeño chiles (from 12-oz jar)
- 2 tablespoons finely chopped green onions (2 medium)
- ⅛ teaspoon salt
- 1 can Pillsbury refrigerated crescent dinner rolls (8 rolls) or 1 can Pillsbury Crescent Dough Sheet

1 Appetizer: Calories 45; Total Fat 3g (Saturated Fat 1.5g, Trans Fat 0g); Cholesterol 5mg; Sodium 80mg; Total Carbohydrate 3g (Dietary Fiber 0g); Protein 1g **Exchanges:** ½ Other Carbohydrate, ½ Fat **Carbohydrate Choices:** 0

Easy Success Tip

For a different flavor, swap finely chopped, crisply cooked bacon for the green onion!

1 Heat oven to 375°F. In small bowl, mix all ingredients except dough until well blended; set aside.

2 If using crescent rolls: Unroll dough on work surface or cutting board; separate into 2 long rectangles, firmly pressing perforations to seal. If using dough sheet: Unroll dough on work surface or cutting board; cut into 2 long rectangles.

3 Spread half of cream cheese mixture on each rectangle to within ½ inch of edges. Starting with long side, roll up rectangle; press seam to seal. Cut each roll into 16 slices; place slices, cut side down, on ungreased cookie sheet.

4 Bake 14 to 16 minutes or until light golden brown. Immediately remove from cookie sheet to serving plate. Serve warm.

loaded potato pinwheels

prep time: 20 Minutes • **start to finish:** 45 Minutes • 28 appetizers

- 1 bag (11.8 oz) frozen backyard grilled potatoes
- 1¼ cups finely shredded sharp Cheddar cheese (5 oz)
- ½ cup cooked real bacon bits or pieces (from a jar or package)
- 3 tablespoons milk
- 1 can Pillsbury refrigerated Crescent Dough Sheet or 1 can Pillsbury refrigerated crescent dinner rolls (8 rolls)
- ⅓ cup sour cream
- 2 tablespoons finely chopped green onions (2 medium)

1 Heat oven 350°F. Spray 2 large cookie sheets with cooking spray.

2 Microwave frozen potatoes 3 to 4 minutes to thaw. In medium bowl, mash potatoes with fork, leaving some small pieces. Stir in cheese, ⅓ cup of the bacon and the milk until well blended.

3 If using dough sheet: Unroll dough on cutting board; press into 14x8-inch rectangle. If using crescent rolls: Unroll dough on cutting board; press into 14x8-inch rectangle, firmly pressing perforations to seal. Cut into 2 (14x4-inch) rectangles. Spread half of potato mixture on each rectangle to within ¼ inch of long edges. Starting with long side, roll up rectangle tightly; pinch seam to seal. Using serrated knife, cut each roll into 14 slices. Place slices, cut sides up, on cookie sheets.

4 Bake 17 to 21 minutes or until golden brown. Immediately remove from cookie sheets to serving plate. Top each pinwheel with sour cream, onions and remaining bacon. Serve warm.

1 Appetizer: Calories 70; Total Fat 4.5g (Saturated Fat 2g; Trans Fat 0g); Cholesterol 10mg; Sodium 200mg; Total Carbohydrate 6g (Dietary Fiber 0g); Protein 3g **Exchanges:** ½ Other Carbohydrate, ½ High-Fat Meat **Carbohydrate Choices:** ½

mediterranean pita bites

prep time: 30 Minutes • **start to finish:** 1 Hour 30 Minutes • 24 appetizers

- 1 can Pillsbury refrigerated crusty French loaf
- 6 teaspoons olive oil
- 1 can (15 oz) chickpeas or garbanzo beans, undrained
- 2 cups small fresh cauliflower florets
- 1 small red or orange bell pepper, cut into 1-inch strips
- ½ teaspoon ground cumin
- ½ teaspoon garam masala
- ½ teaspoon salt
- ⅓ cup olive oil
- 2 tablespoons chopped fresh cilantro

1 Heat oven to 375°F. Spray 2 cookie sheets with cooking spray. Using serrated knife, cut loaf into 24 (½-inch) slices. Place slices, cut side down, 2 inches apart on cookie sheets. Press into 2-inch rounds. Brush with 2 teaspoons of the oil.

2 Bake 11 to 15 minutes or until edges are golden brown and crisp. Remove from cookie sheets to cooling racks.

3 Increase oven temperature to 425°F. Drain chickpeas, reserving ¼ cup liquid; rinse and drain chickpeas. In medium bowl, toss chickpeas, cauliflower, bell pepper, cumin, garam masala, salt and remaining 4 teaspoons oil until vegetables are thoroughly coated. Spread in single layer in ungreased 15x10x1-inch pan.

4 Bake uncovered 20 to 30 minutes, stirring once, until cauliflower is golden brown and vegetables are tender. Cool 15 minutes.

5 Reserve ¾ cup vegetables for topping. Place remaining vegetables in food processor; add ⅓ cup oil and reserved ¼ cup chickpea liquid. Cover; process about 1 minute, scraping down side once with rubber spatula, until smooth.

6 To assemble, spread 1 tablespoon vegetable mixture on each pita. Divide reserved vegetables evenly among pitas, pressing gently into vegetable mixture. Sprinkle with cilantro.

1 Appetizer: Calories 90; Total Fat 5g (Saturated Fat 0.5g, Trans Fat 0g); Cholesterol 0mg; Sodium 140mg; Total Carbohydrate 10g (Dietary Fiber 1g); Protein 2g **Exchanges:** ½ Starch, 1 Fat **Carbohydrate Choices:** ½

tropical crab rangoon appetizers

prep time: 20 Minutes • **start to finish:** 55 Minutes • 12 appetizers

- **1 can Pillsbury refrigerated classic pizza crust**
- **1 package (8 oz) cream cheese, softened**
- **¼ cup mayonnaise or salad dressing**
- **½ teaspoon Chinese hot mustard, if desired**
- **¼ teaspoon garlic salt**
- **1 can (8 oz) sliced water chestnuts, drained, coarsely chopped**
- **1 can (6 oz) lump crabmeat, drained**
- **¼ cup pineapple topping**
- **2 cups shredded Monterey Jack cheese (8 oz)**
- **4 medium green onions, chopped (¼ cup)**

1 Heat oven to 400°F for dark or nonstick pan (425°F for all other pans). Spray large cookie sheet or 16-inch pizza pan with cooking spray.

2 Unroll dough on cookie sheet; starting at center, press dough into 17x12-inch rectangle. Bake 7 to 9 minutes or just until crust is light golden brown.

3 Meanwhile, in large bowl, beat cream cheese, mayonnaise, mustard and garlic salt with electric mixer on medium speed until smooth. Stir in water chestnuts and crabmeat, being careful to break up crabmeat as little as possible.

4 Spread crabmeat mixture over partially baked crust to within 1 inch of edges. Spoon small spoonfuls of pineapple topping over crabmeat mixture; spread evenly. Sprinkle with Monterey Jack cheese and onions.

5 Bake 12 to 15 minutes or until cheese is bubbly and crust is golden brown. Cool 5 to 10 minutes. Cut into 4 rows by 3 rows. Serve warm.

1 Appetizer: Calories 290; Total Fat 17g (Saturated Fat 9g; Trans Fat 0g); Cholesterol 50mg; Sodium 480mg; Total Carbohydrate 23g (Dietary Fiber 0g); Protein 11g **Exchanges:** 1 Starch, ½ Other Carbohydrate, 1 High-Fat Meat, 1½ Fat **Carbohydrate Choices:** 1½

Easy Success Tips

Substitute ground mustard for the Chinese hot mustard.

If you can't find pineapple ice cream topping, try peach or apricot preserves instead.

pastrami-pretzel bites

prep time: 30 Minutes • **start to finish:** 55 Minutes • 15 appetizers

- **1 can Pillsbury Grands! Homestyle refrigerated buttermilk biscuits (5 biscuits)**
- **3 tablespoons baking soda**
- **2 teaspoons coarse (kosher or sea) salt**
- **2 teaspoons butter, melted**
- **¼ lb sliced pastrami (from deli), finely chopped**
- **¼ cup red tart cherry preserves**
- **¼ teaspoon chili powder**
- **5 tablespoons honey mustard**

1 Heat oven to 425°F. Line large cookie sheet with cooking parchment paper. In 10-inch skillet, heat 3 cups water to boiling over high heat.

2 Meanwhile, separate dough into 5 biscuits; cut each biscuit into 3 wedges. Roll each wedge into 6-inch rope; tie in knot. Add baking soda to boiling water; reduce heat to medium. Carefully place 5 biscuit knots into boiling water; cook 15 seconds on each side. Using slotted spoon to drain excess water, transfer biscuit knots to cookie sheet, placing 1 inch apart. Repeat with remaining biscuit knots. Sprinkle biscuit knots with salt.

3 Bake 11 to 15 minutes or until deep golden brown. Brush tops with butter; cool 10 minutes. Meanwhile, in small bowl, mix pastrami, preserves and chili powder.

4 Cut each warm pretzel bite horizontally in half. Spread ½ teaspoon mustard on each cut side. Spoon 1 tablespoon pastrami mixture onto each pretzel bite bottom. Cover with pretzel bite tops; secure with toothpicks.

1 Appetizer: Calories 90; Total Fat 3g (Saturated Fat 1.5g; Trans Fat 0g); Cholesterol 5mg; Sodium 400mg; Total Carbohydrate 13g (Dietary Fiber 0g); Protein 2g **Exchanges:** ½ Starch, ½ Other Carbohydrate, ½ Fat **Carbohydrate Choices:** 1

razzle-dazzle beef bites

prep time: 20 Minutes • **start to finish:** 40 Minutes • 16 appetizers

- 1 can Pillsbury Place 'N Bake™ refrigerated crescent rounds or 1 can Pillsbury refrigerated crescent dinner rolls (8 rolls)
- 3 oz (from 8-oz package) cream cheese, softened
- ½ teaspoon lemon-pepper seasoning
- ½ cup red raspberry preserves
- 1 tablespoon prepared horseradish
- 1 teaspoon Dijon mustard
- 3 oz shaved cooked roast beef (from deli)
- 1 tablespoon chopped fresh parsley

1 Heat oven to 375°F. Remove dough from can but do not separate or unroll. Using serrated knife, cut roll into 16 slices; carefully separate slices. Place 1 slice in each of 16 ungreased regular-size muffin cups. Bake 8 to 10 minutes or until golden brown.

2 Immediately press back of rounded teaspoon into center of each baked round to make indentation. Remove from pans to cooling racks; cool 10 minutes.

3 Meanwhile, in small bowl, mix cream cheese and lemon-pepper seasoning. In another small bowl, mix preserves, horseradish and mustard.

4 Spread 1 teaspoon cream cheese mixture into each cooled baked round; top each with ½ teaspoon preserves mixture. Divide beef evenly among appetizers; top each with 1 rounded teaspoon preserves mixture. Sprinkle with parsley.

1 Appetizer: Calories 110; Total Fat 5g (Saturated Fat 2g; Trans Fat 1g); Cholesterol 10mg; Sodium 200mg; Total Carbohydrate 13g (Dietary Fiber 0g); Protein 2g **Exchanges:** ½ Starch, ½ Other Carbohydrate, 1 Fat **Carbohydrate Choices:** 1

creamy corn-filled sweet peppers

prep time: 30 Minutes • **start to finish:** 1 Hour • 22 appetizers

- 1 bag (11.8 oz) frozen honey-roasted sweet corn
- 1 package (8 oz) cream cheese, softened
- 1 cup grated Parmesan cheese
- 1 teaspoon Italian seasoning
- 11 mini sweet peppers (3 to 4 inches long), cut in half lengthwise leaving stem attached, seeded
- 1 can Pillsbury refrigerated Crescent Dough Sheet or 1 can Pillsbury refrigerated crescent dinner rolls (8 rolls)
- 3 tablespoons butter, melted

1 Heat oven to 375°F. Line large cookie sheet with cooking parchment paper. Microwave corn as directed on bag. Cut open bag; cool 10 minutes.

2 In large bowl, beat cream cheese with electric mixer on medium speed until smooth. Add corn, ½ cup of the Parmesan cheese and ½ teaspoon of the Italian seasoning; mix well. Spoon cream cheese mixture into large resealable food-storage plastic bag. Cut ½ inch off corner of bag; squeeze bag to pipe filling into each pepper half.

3 If using dough sheet: Unroll dough on cutting board; press into 11x9-inch rectangle. If using crescent rolls: Unroll dough on cutting board; press into 11x9-inch rectangle, firmly pressing perforations to seal. With pizza cutter or knife, cut dough into 22 (9x½-inch) strips.

4 Wrap 1 dough strip around each pepper, from stem to tip. Place peppers, filling side up, on cookie sheet, tucking ends of dough under pepper.

5 Bake 12 to 18 minutes or until golden brown. In small bowl, mix butter and remaining ½ teaspoon Italian seasoning. Brush mixture over peppers; sprinkle evenly with remaining ½ cup Parmesan cheese. Serve warm.

1 Appetizer: Calories 130; Total Fat 8g (Saturated Fat 4.5g; Trans Fat 0g); Cholesterol 20mg; Sodium 250mg; Total Carbohydrate 10g (Dietary Fiber 1g); Protein 4g **Exchanges:** ½ Starch, ½ Vegetable, 1½ Fat **Carbohydrate Choices:** ½

Easy Success Tip

Unbaked appetizers can be covered and refrigerated up to 2 hours before baking. Add a few extra minutes to the bake time, if necessary.

tiny ham-and-pineapple pot pies

prep time: 40 Minutes • **start to finish:** 1 Hour • 16 appetizers

- ½ cup finely chopped cooked ham
- ½ cup finely shredded Swiss cheese (2 oz)
- ½ cup crushed pineapple (from 8-oz can), well drained
- 1 tablespoon finely chopped green onion (1 medium)
- ½ teaspoon ground mustard
- 1 box Pillsbury refrigerated pie crusts, softened as directed on box
- 1 egg, beaten
- 1 teaspoon sesame seed, if desired

1 Heat oven to 450°F (425°F for dark or nonstick pans). In small bowl, mix ham, cheese, pineapple, onion and mustard; set aside.

2 Unroll pie crusts on work surface. Cut 8 (3-inch) rounds and 8 (2-inch) rounds from each crust, rerolling crusts if necessary. In 16 ungreased mini muffin cups, press 3-inch rounds in bottoms and up sides so edges of crusts extend slightly over sides of cups.

3 Spoon about 1 rounded tablespoon ham mixture into each crust-lined cup. Brush crust edges lightly with beaten egg.

4 Cut small vent in each 2-inch crust round. Place 1 round over filling in each cup; press crust edges together, pushing toward cup so crust does not extend over side. Brush top crusts with beaten egg. Sprinkle with sesame seed.

5 Bake 10 to 14 minutes or until golden brown. Remove from muffin cups. Cool 5 minutes. Serve warm.

1 Appetizer: Calories 130; Total Fat 9g (Saturated Fat 3g, Trans Fat 2.5g); Cholesterol 15mg; Sodium 200mg; Total Carbohydrate 10g (Dietary Fiber 0g); Protein 3g **Exchanges:** ½ Other Carbohydrate, ½ Lean Meat, 1½ Fat **Carbohydrate Choices:** ½

asian pork dumplings

prep time: 50 Minutes • **start to finish:** 1 Hour 20 Minutes • 48 appetizers

- 1¼ lbs lean ground pork
- 1 can (8 oz) sliced or whole water chestnuts, drained, coarsely chopped
- 1 box (9 oz) frozen chopped spinach, thawed, squeezed to drain
- 12 medium green onions, thinly sliced (about ¾ cup)
- 2 tablespoons soy sauce
- 1 teaspoon granulated garlic or garlic powder
- ¾ teaspoon ground ginger
- ¾ teaspoon white pepper or black pepper
- 2 eggs
- 2 cans Pillsbury Grands! Flaky Layers Original refrigerated biscuits (8 biscuits each)
- 1½ cups sweet-and-sour sauce or sweet-spicy chili sauce

1 Heat oven to 350°F. In large bowl, mix all ingredients except biscuits and sweet-and-sour sauce.

2 Remove 1 can of biscuits from refrigerator just before filling (keep remaining can of biscuits refrigerated). Separate dough into 8 biscuits; separate each biscuit into 3 layers. Press each layer into 3½-inch round, being careful not to tear dough.

3 Spoon 1 rounded tablespoon of pork filling onto center of each dough round. Bring all sides of dough up over filling, stretching gently if necessary, and gather in center above filling to form a dumpling; press gathered dough to seal. Place 2 inches apart on ungreased large cookie sheet. Repeat with remaining biscuits and filling to make 24 more dumplings.

4 Bake 17 to 27 minutes or until thermometer inserted in center reads 160°F* and sides and tops of dumplings are golden brown. Serve warm with sweet-and-sour sauce.

***Due to the natural nitrate content of certain ingredients such as onions, the pork filling may remain pink even though pork is cooked to 160°F.**

1 Appetizer: Calories 100; Total Fat 5g (Saturated Fat 1.5g; Trans Fat 1g); Cholesterol 15mg; Sodium 260mg; Total Carbohydrate 11g (Dietary Fiber 0g); Protein 4g **Exchanges:** ½ Starch, ½ High-Fat Meat **Carbohydrate Choices:** 1

Easy Success Tip

Unbaked dumplings can be covered and refrigerated up to 2 hours before baking. Add a few extra minutes to the bake time, if necessary.

mango, prosciutto and goat cheese appetizer pizza

prep time: 30 Minutes • **start to finish:** 40 Minutes • 24 appetizers

- 1 can Pillsbury refrigerated classic pizza crust
- 1 tablespoon olive oil
- 1 medium onion, chopped (½ cup)
- 1 firm ripe mango, seed removed, peeled and cut into ¼-inch pieces (1 cup)
- ⅓ cup orange marmalade
- 1 tablespoon Dijon mustard
- 2 tablespoons balsamic vinegar
- 1 to 2 teaspoons soy sauce
- 4 oz thinly sliced prosciutto
- 1 cup shredded mozzarella cheese (4 oz)
- 1 cup crumbled goat (chèvre) cheese (4 oz)

1 Heat oven to 400°F for dark or nonstick pan (425°F for all other pans). Spray large cookie sheet with cooking spray.

2 Unroll dough on cookie sheet; starting at center, press dough into 15x10-inch rectangle. Bake 8 to 10 minutes or until edges just begin to brown.

3 Meanwhile, in 10-inch skillet, heat oil over medium heat. Cook onion in oil about 5 minutes, stirring occasionally, until softened and starting to brown. Add ½ cup of the mango. Cook 3 minutes, stirring frequently. Stir in marmalade, mustard, vinegar and soy sauce. Cook 2 to 3 minutes, stirring frequently, until mixture thickens and most of liquid is absorbed.

4 Spread mango-onion mixture over partially baked crust. Top with prosciutto; sprinkle with cheeses.

5 Bake 8 to 10 minutes or until crust is golden brown and cheese is melted. Sprinkle with remaining ½ cup mango. Cut into 6 rows by 4 rows.

1 Appetizer: Calories 110; Total Fat 4g (Saturated Fat 2g; Trans Fat 0g); Cholesterol 10mg; Sodium 260mg; Total Carbohydrate 13g (Dietary Fiber 0g); Protein 5g **Exchanges:** ½ Starch, ½ Other Carbohydrate, ½ High-Fat Meat **Carbohydrate Choices:** 1

Easy Success Tip

For a change in flavor that has a bit more tang, substitute fontina cheese for the mozzarella.

Bake-Off® Contest 47, 2014 | **Rebecca Farias-Insco** | Bartlett, IL

brussels sprouts–reuben flatbread

prep time: 15 Minutes • **start to finish:** 25 Minutes • 24 appetizers

- 1 can Pillsbury refrigerated thin pizza crust
- 1½ teaspoons caraway seed, ground
- 1 bag (11 oz) frozen Brussels sprouts with sea salt and cracked pepper
- 1 lb shaved corned beef (from deli)
- 1½ cups shredded Swiss cheese (6 oz)
- ½ cup Thousand Island dressing

1 Heat oven to 400°F for dark or nonstick pan (425°F for all other pans). Unroll dough in ungreased nonstick 15x10x1-inch pan. Starting at center, press dough to edges of pan.

2 Sprinkle caraway seed over dough; press gently into crust. Bake 6 to 7 minutes or until edges of crust begin to turn light golden brown.

3 Meanwhile, microwave frozen Brussels sprouts as directed on bag. Drain; coarsely chop.

4 Arrange corned beef on partially baked crust; top with Brussels sprouts and cheese. Bake 7 to 10 minutes or until cheese is melted. Cut into 6 rows by 4 rows. Drizzle with dressing. Serve warm.

1 Appetizer: Calories 120; Total Fat 6g (Saturated Fat 2g; Trans Fat 0g); Cholesterol 20mg; Sodium 450mg; Total Carbohydrate 8g (Dietary Fiber 0g); Protein 7g **Exchanges:** ½ Other Carbohydrate, 1 Lean Meat, ½ Fat **Carbohydrate Choices:** ½

Easy Success Tip

To grind caraway seed, use a spice grinder or place seed in a mortar and pestle. Or, place seed in resealable food-storage plastic bag and crush with meat mallet or rolling pin.

Bake-Off® Contest 47, 2014 | **JoAnn Belack** | Bradenton, FL

pepper jack–salsa flatbread with an italian twist

prep time: 10 Minutes • **start to finish:** 35 Minutes • 12 appetizers

- 1 can Pillsbury refrigerated thin pizza crust
- 2 cups shredded reduced-fat mozzarella cheese (8 oz)
- 2 cups shredded pepper Jack cheese (8 oz)
- 1 container (16 oz) refrigerated salsa, drained (about 1 cup)
- ½ teaspoon Italian seasoning
- ½ teaspoon garlic powder

1 Heat oven to 400°F for dark or nonstick pan (425°F for all other pans). Line large cookie sheet with cooking parchment paper.

2 Unroll dough on cookie sheet; starting at center, press dough into 12-inch square. With pizza cutter or kitchen scissors, cut dough in half. Pinch dough around edges of each half to form rim, crimping edges as desired. Bake 6 minutes.

3 Sprinkle 1¾ cups of the mozzarella cheese and the pepper Jack cheese evenly over partially baked flatbreads to within ½ inch of edges. Spoon and gently spread salsa over cheese. Sprinkle with remaining ¼ cup mozzarella cheese, the Italian seasoning and garlic powder.

4 Bake 10 to 15 minutes or until crust is golden brown and cheese is melted. Cut each flatbread crosswise into thirds; cut each third in half diagonally to make 12 triangles.

1 Appetizer: Calories 200; Total Fat 11g (Saturated Fat 4g; Trans Fat 0g); Cholesterol 25mg; Sodium 510mg; Total Carbohydrate 15g (Dietary Fiber 0g); Protein 12g **Exchanges:** 1 Other Carbohydrate, ½ Lean Meat, 1 High-Fat Meat, ½ Fat **Carbohydrate Choices:** 1

Easy Success Tip

The salsa is drained in this recipe to keep all the yummy flavor of the chunky ingredients but not the liquid, which would make the flatbread soggy. Save the liquid to make zesty Bloody Marys or add zip to tomato juice!

italian meatball–stuffed crescent ring

prep time: 15 Minutes • **start to finish:** 45 Minutes • 16 servings

- 24 frozen cooked Italian-style meatballs, 1 inch (from 16-oz bag), thawed
- 1½ cups marinara sauce
- 1 cup shredded mozzarella cheese (4 oz)
- 2 cans Pillsbury refrigerated crescent dinner rolls (8 rolls each)
- 1 tablespoon butter, melted
- 1 tablespoon grated Parmesan cheese

Easy Success Tips

Italian cheese blend can be substituted for the mozzarella.

Try serving warmed Alfredo sauce along with or instead of the marinara sauce.

1 Heat oven to 375°F. Cut each meatball in half. In large bowl, gently stir together meatballs, ½ cup of the marinara sauce and the mozzarella cheese.

2 Unroll both cans of dough; separate into 8 rectangles. On ungreased large cookie sheet, arrange rectangles in ring so short sides form 5-inch square in center. (Dough will overlap; edges of rectangles may hang over edges of cookie sheet.)

3 Spoon meatball mixture onto bottoms of rectangles (closest to center of ring); each rectangle should have 6 meatball halves. Bring opposite side of each rectangle up over filling, tucking under bottom layer of dough to secure it. Repeat around ring until entire filling is enclosed. Gently separate dough perforations on top until filling peeks through. Brush dough with melted butter; sprinkle with Parmesan cheese.

4 Bake 20 to 25 minutes or until dough is golden brown and thoroughly baked. Cool 5 minutes before cutting. Just before serving, in small microwavable bowl, microwave remaining 1 cup marinara sauce uncovered on Medium-High (70%) 1 to 2 minutes or until hot. Serve with crescent ring.

1 Serving: Calories 390; Total Fat 21g (Saturated Fat 9g; Trans Fat 0g); Cholesterol 55mg; Sodium 940mg; Total Carbohydrate 34g (Dietary Fiber 1g); Protein 17g **Exchanges:** 1 Starch, 1 Other Carbohydrate, ½ Vegetable, 1 Medium-Fat Meat, 1 High-Fat Meat, 1½ Fat **Carbohydrate Choices:** 2

buffalo chicken crescent ring

prep time: 15 Minutes • **start to finish:** 45 Minutes • 16 servings

- 4 oz (half of 8-oz package) cream cheese, softened
- ¼ cup Buffalo wing sauce
- 2½ cups chopped cooked chicken (½-inch pieces)
- 1 cup shredded Monterey Jack cheese (4 oz)
- 2 cans Pillsbury refrigerated crescent dinner rolls (8 rolls each)
- ⅓ cup crumbled blue cheese

1 Heat oven to 375°F. In medium bowl, mix cream cheese and Buffalo wing sauce until smooth. Add chicken and Monterey Jack cheese; mix just until combined.

2 Unroll both cans of dough; separate into 16 triangles. On ungreased large cookie sheet, arrange triangles in ring so short sides form 5-inch circle in center. (Dough will overlap; points of triangles may hang over edges of cookie sheet. Dough ring should look like a sun.)

3 Spoon chicken mixture onto bottoms of triangles (closest to center of ring). Top with blue cheese. Bring point of each triangle up over filling, tucking under bottom layer of dough to secure it. Repeat around ring until entire filling is enclosed (some filling might show a little). Gently separate dough on top until filling peeks through.

4 Bake 20 to 25 minutes or until dough is golden brown and thoroughly baked. Cool 5 minutes before cutting. Serve with dressing and celery.

1 Serving: Calories 200; Total Fat 12g (Saturated Fat 6g; Trans Fat 0g); Cholesterol 35mg; Sodium 420mg; Total Carbohydrate 12g (Dietary Fiber 0g); Protein 11g **Exchanges:** 1 Other Carbohydrate, 1 Very Lean Meat, ½ High-Fat Meat, 1½ Fat **Carbohydrate Choices:** 1

Easy Success Tips

Turn this spicy appetizer ring into an easy dinner by cutting into 8 servings. Serve with a cool tossed salad.

Serve with the classic Buffalo wing accompaniments, blue cheese dip and celery sticks, if desired.

mini hot dogs in a bun

prep time: 45 Minutes • **start to finish:** 1 Hour 15 Minutes • 32 sandwiches

- 1 can Pillsbury refrigerated crusty French loaf
- 1 egg white, beaten
- 2 teaspoons sesame seed, if desired
- 32 cocktail-size hot dogs or smoked link sausages
- ¼ cup spicy brown mustard
- 1 cup creamy coleslaw (from deli)
- ¾ cup sliced pepperoncini peppers (bottled Italian peppers)

1 Heat oven to 350°F. Spray 2 large cookie sheets with cooking spray.

2 With serrated knife, cut loaf into 32 pieces. Roll each dough piece into a ball; shape into 2½-inch log. Place 1 inch apart on cookie sheets. Brush with egg white. Sprinkle with sesame seed.

3 Bake 18 to 22 minutes or until golden brown. Remove from cookie sheets to cooling racks; cool 5 minutes.

4 Meanwhile, cook hot dogs as directed on package. Cover to keep warm.

5 Cut each mini bun lengthwise in half to within ¼ inch of bottom. Spread about ½ teaspoon mustard on one cut side of each bun; place hot dogs in buns. Top evenly with coleslaw and pepper slices.

1 Sandwich: Calories 70; Total Fat 4.5g (Saturated Fat 1.5g, Trans Fat 0g); Cholesterol 5mg; Sodium 230mg; Total Carbohydrate 6g (Dietary Fiber 0g); Protein 2g **Exchanges:** ½ Starch, 1 Fat **Carbohydrate Choices:** ½

Easy Success Tip

For more traditional hot dogs, top with ketchup, yellow mustard and pickle relish.

CHAPTER 2

sandwiches

thai chicken subs

prep time: 40 Minutes • **start to finish:** 40 Minutes • 6 sandwiches

- 2 cans Pillsbury refrigerated crusty French loaf
- 1 cup coleslaw mix (from 16-oz bag)
- 1 small red onion, halved lengthwise, cut into thin wedges (1 cup)
- 1 medium red bell pepper, cut into ⅛-inch strips (1 cup)
- ½ medium hothouse (seedless) cucumber, cut into 2x¼x¼-inch pieces (1 cup)
- ¼ cup chopped fresh cilantro
- ¾ cup soy-teriyaki blend or ¾ cup stir-fry sauce plus 2 teaspoons sesame seed
- ¾ cup seasoned rice vinegar
- 2 tablespoons packed brown sugar
- 1½ teaspoons hot chili sauce
- ¼ cup creamy peanut butter
- 1 tablespoon vegetable oil
- 1½ lbs uncooked chicken breast tenders (not breaded)

1 Heat oven to 350°F. Spray large cookie sheet with cooking spray. Place loaves, seam side down and 3 inches apart, on cookie sheet. Using sharp knife, cut 5 diagonal ½-inch-deep slashes on top of dough. Bake 26 to 30 minutes or until golden brown.

2 Meanwhile, in medium bowl, toss coleslaw mix, onion, bell pepper, cucumber and cilantro. In 2-cup measuring cup, beat ½ cup of the soy-teriyaki blend, ½ cup of the rice vinegar, 1 tablespoon of the brown sugar and 1 teaspoon of the chili sauce with whisk. Pour over coleslaw mixture; toss to combine. Set aside, stirring occasionally.

3 In 1-quart saucepan, stir together peanut butter and remaining ¼ cup soy-teriyaki blend, ¼ cup rice vinegar, 1 tablespoon brown sugar and ½ teaspoon chili sauce. Cook over medium heat 4 to 5 minutes, stirring occasionally, until smooth. Set aside.

4 In 12-inch skillet, heat oil over medium-high heat. Cook chicken in oil 7 to 10 minutes, turning once, until no longer pink in center. Add peanut sauce; stir to coat. Remove from heat.

5 Cut each loaf crosswise into thirds; cut each piece of bread in half lengthwise down center to within ½ inch of bottom. Spoon chicken mixture evenly into bread. With slotted spoon, top each sub with about ½ cup coleslaw mixture. Serve any remaining sauce for dipping.

1 Sandwich: Calories 520; Total Fat 12g (Saturated Fat 2.5g; Trans Fat 0g); Cholesterol 50mg; Sodium 1860mg; Total Carbohydrate 67g (Dietary Fiber 2g); Protein 35g **Exchanges:** 3 Starch, 1 Other Carbohydrate, 1 Vegetable, 3 Very Lean Meat, ½ High-Fat Meat, 1 Fat **Carbohydrate Choices:** 4½

apricot-curry chicken sandwiches

prep time: 45 Minutes • **start to finish:** 1 Hour 5 Minutes • 8 sandwiches

- 1 tablespoon curry powder
- ½ teaspoon ground cinnamon
- ½ teaspoon ground nutmeg
- ¼ teaspoon ground cloves
- 1 teaspoon salt
- 4 boneless skinless chicken breasts (about 6 oz each)
- 4 tablespoons vegetable oil
- ½ cup finely chopped red onion
- ¼ teaspoon crushed red pepper flakes
- 1 jalapeño chile, seeded, finely chopped
- 1 jar (10.25 oz) reduced-sugar apricot preserves (1 cup)
- Dash salt
- 2 cans Pillsbury Crescent Dough Sheet
- 2 slices (¾ oz each) Cheddar cheese, cut into quarters
- ½ cup sliced almonds, toasted*
- 1 egg
- 1 tablespoon water

*To toast almonds, sprinkle in ungreased skillet. Cook over medium heat 5 to 7 minutes, stirring frequently until almonds begin to brown, then stirring constantly until light brown. Remove from skillet to plate to cool.

1 In small bowl, mix curry powder, cinnamon, nutmeg, cloves and 1 teaspoon salt. Cut each chicken breast in half crosswise to make total of 8 equal portions. Coat chicken evenly with seasoning mixture.

2 In 12-inch nonstick skillet, heat 3 tablespoons of the oil over medium-high heat. Cook chicken in oil 6 to 8 minutes, turning once, until lightly browned. Remove from heat.

3 In 2-quart saucepan, heat remaining 1 tablespoon oil over medium-high heat. Cook onion, pepper flakes and chile in oil 4 to 6 minutes, stirring frequently, until onion is tender. Reduce heat to medium. Stir in preserves; cook about 5 minutes or until heated. Add dash salt; remove from heat. Cool slightly.

4 Heat oven to 375°F. Line cookie sheet with cooking parchment paper. Unroll dough sheets on work surface. Cut each sheet into 4 rectangles. On center of each rectangle, place 1 cheese piece; top with 1 teaspoon preserves mixture, 1 teaspoon almonds and 1 chicken piece.

5 In small bowl, beat egg and water; brush on edges of dough. Bring up dough over filling; press edges to seal. Place, seam side down, on cookie sheet. Brush tops with remaining egg mixture; sprinkle with any remaining almonds.

6 Bake 12 to 18 minutes or until golden brown. Serve warm with remaining preserves mixture.

1 Sandwich: Calories 530; Total Fat 24g (Saturated Fat 6g; Trans Fat 0g); Cholesterol 80mg; Sodium 860mg; Total Carbohydrate 52g (Dietary Fiber 2g); Protein 26g **Exchanges:** 2½ Starch, 1 Other Carbohydrate, 2½ Lean Meat, 3 Fat **Carbohydrate Choices:** 3½

Bake-Off® Contest 46, 2013 | **Marie Valdes** | Brandon, FL

honey chicken and corn rafts

prep time: 30 Minutes • **start to finish:** 30 Minutes • 6 servings

- 4 tablespoons olive oil
- 1 can Pillsbury refrigerated thin pizza crust
- 1½ lbs boneless skinless chicken breasts, cut into ¾-inch cubes
- 2 tablespoons honey
- ¼ teaspoon salt
- ¼ teaspoon pepper
- 1 bag (11.8 oz) frozen honey-roasted sweet corn
- 6 tablespoons cooked real bacon pieces (from jar or package)
- 1 cup baby arugula
- ⅛ teaspoon salt

1 Heat oven to 400°F for dark or nonstick pan (425°F for all other pans). Brush large cookie sheet with 1 tablespoon of the oil.

2 Unroll dough on cookie sheet. Cut dough into 6 squares. Roll up edges of each dough square, forming ¼-inch rim; pinch corners to look like rafts. Bake 9 to 11 minutes or until golden brown.

3 Meanwhile, in medium bowl, toss chicken with honey, ¼ teaspoon salt and ⅛ teaspoon of the pepper. In 12-inch nonstick skillet, heat 2 tablespoons of the oil over medium heat. Add chicken mixture; cook 10 to 15 minutes, stirring occasionally, until chicken is no longer pink in center.

4 Microwave corn as directed on bag. Add corn and bacon to chicken; cook 1 minute longer or until thoroughly heated.

5 In small bowl, toss arugula with ⅛ teaspoon salt, remaining ⅛ teaspoon pepper and remaining 1 tablespoon oil. Spoon chicken mixture onto rafts; top with arugula.

1 Serving: Calories 470; Total Fat 20g (Saturated Fat 3.5g; Trans Fat 0g); Cholesterol 80mg; Sodium 850mg; Total Carbohydrate 39g (Dietary Fiber 2g); Protein 34g **Exchanges:** 2 Starch, ½ Other Carbohydrate, 4 Very Lean Meat, 3½ Fat **Carbohydrate Choices:** 2½

Bake-Off® Contest 44, 2010 | **Laureen Pittman** | Riverside, CA

herb chicken sliders with raspberry mustard

prep time: 30 Minutes • **start to finish:** 55 Minutes • 10 sliders

- 1 can Pillsbury refrigerated crusty French loaf
- 1 egg
- 1 teaspoon water
- ½ cup seedless red raspberry jam
- 2 tablespoons Dijon mustard
- 2 teaspoons whole-grain Dijon mustard, if desired
- 1¼ lbs ground chicken or turkey
- 4 medium green onions, chopped (¼ cup)
- 2 tablespoons chopped fresh Italian (flat-leaf) parsley
- 1 teaspoon dried tarragon leaves
- ½ teaspoon garlic powder
- 1 tablespoon vegetable oil
- 1 bag (5 oz) mixed baby salad greens
- 1 medium tomato, thinly sliced

1 Heat oven to 350°F. Spray 10 regular-size muffin cups with cooking spray. Cut loaf of dough crosswise into 10 slices. Place each slice, cut side up, in muffin cup. In small bowl, beat egg and water; brush over dough.

2 Bake 16 to 22 minutes or until tops are golden brown. Remove from pan to cooling rack; cool 5 minutes.

3 Meanwhile, in small bowl, beat jam and mustards with fork or whisk until smooth; set aside.

4 In medium bowl, mix chicken, onions, parsley, tarragon and garlic powder. Shape mixture into 10 patties, about ½ inch thick. In 12-inch nonstick skillet, heat oil over medium-high heat. Add patties; cook 6 to 10 minutes, turning once, until thermometer inserted in center reads 165°F.

5 Cut each bun horizontally in half. Spoon 1 teaspoon raspberry mustard onto cut sides of each bun. Place burgers on bun bottoms; top with small amount of greens. Cover with bun tops. Garnish with tomato and remaining greens. Serve with remaining raspberry mustard.

1 Slider: Calories 210; Total Fat 6g (Saturated Fat 1.5g; Trans Fat 0g); Cholesterol 50mg; Sodium 290mg; Total Carbohydrate 27g (Dietary Fiber 0g); Protein 10g **Exchanges:** 1 Starch, ½ Other Carbohydrate, ½ Vegetable, 1 Lean Meat, ½ Fat **Carbohydrate Choices:** 2

turkey and cherry sandwich minis

prep time: 20 Minutes • **start to finish:** 40 Minutes • 16 sandwiches

- **1 can Pillsbury refrigerated crusty French loaf**
- **2 slices bacon, finely chopped**
- **3 tablespoons mayonnaise**
- **¼ cup crumbled blue cheese (1 oz)**
- **¼ cup cherry preserves**
- **½ lb thinly sliced smoked turkey breast (from deli)**
- **4 large leaves red lettuce, cut into quarters**

1 Heat oven to 350°F. Spray large cookie sheet with cooking spray.

2 Place dough on work surface. Flatten loaf to 18 inches long and 2 inches thick. Cut in half lengthwise. With serrated knife, cut each half into 8 slices to make 16 buns. Place on cookie sheet. Bake 17 to 20 minutes or until golden brown. Remove from cookie sheet to cooling rack; cool 10 minutes.

3 Meanwhile, in 8-inch nonstick skillet, cook bacon over medium-high heat 3 to 5 minutes, stirring occasionally, until crisp. Drain on paper towel. In small bowl, mix bacon, mayonnaise and blue cheese.

4 Cut each bun in half horizontally to within ¼ inch of other side; open bun to lie flat. On each bun bottom, spread about 1 teaspoon mayonnaise mixture. On each bun top, spread about ¾ teaspoon preserves. Fill buns with turkey and lettuce.

1 Sandwich: Calories 110; Total Fat 4g (Saturated Fat 1g; Trans Fat 0g); Cholesterol 10mg; Sodium 340mg; Total Carbohydrate 13g (Dietary Fiber 0g); Protein 4g **Exchanges:** ½ Starch, ½ Other Carbohydrate, ½ Very Lean Meat, ½ Fat **Carbohydrate Choices:** 1

peppered bacon–wrapped turkey pub sandwiches

prep time: 20 Minutes • **start to finish:** 55 Minutes • 8 sandwiches

- 1 can Pillsbury Grands! Flaky Layers refrigerated Butter Tastin' biscuits (8 biscuits)
- 3 tablespoons chopped green onions (3 medium)
- 4 turkey breast tenderloins (8 oz each)
- 16 slices thick-sliced peppered bacon
- ⅓ cup mayonnaise
- ½ teaspoon garlic powder
- ¼ teaspoon pepper
- 2 cups shredded four-cheese blend (8 oz)

1 Heat oven to 350°F. Line large cookie sheet and 15x10x1-inch pan with cooking parchment paper.

2 Separate dough into 8 biscuits. Brush biscuit tops with water; press onions into biscuit tops. Place 2 inches apart, onion side up, on cookie sheet. Bake 14 to 17 minutes or until golden brown. Remove from cookie sheet to cooling rack. Increase oven temperature to 400°F.

3 Cut each turkey tenderloin crosswise in half to make 8 tenderloin steaks. Wrap 2 slices of bacon in crisscross pattern around each steak. Place in 15x10x1-inch pan. Bake 28 to 30 minutes or until juice of turkey is clear when center of thickest part is cut (165°F) and bacon is cooked.

4 Meanwhile, in small bowl, mix mayonnaise, garlic powder and pepper until well blended. Refrigerate until serving time.

5 Set oven control to broil. Split biscuits; return to cookie sheet, split side up. Sprinkle ¼ cup cheese on split side of each biscuit top. Broil with tops 4 inches from heat 1 to 2 minutes or until biscuits are toasted and cheese is melted. Spread mayonnaise mixture on split sides of biscuit bottoms; top with turkey steaks. Cover with biscuit tops.

1 Sandwich: Calories 530; Total Fat 28g (Saturated Fat 11g; Trans Fat 0g); Cholesterol 120mg; Sodium 1130mg; Total Carbohydrate 27g (Dietary Fiber 0g); Protein 42g
Exchanges: 1 Starch, 1 Other Carbohydrate, 4 Very Lean Meat, 1½ High-Fat Meat, 2½ Fat
Carbohydrate Choices: 2

Bake-Off® Contest 43, 2008 | **Kim Frantz** | Denver, CO

turkey, bacon and brie panini with apricot aioli

prep time: 40 Minutes • **start to finish:** 40 Minutes • 4 sandwiches

- **1 can Pillsbury refrigerated classic pizza crust**
- **8 slices bacon**
- **¼ cup mayonnaise or salad dressing**
- **¼ cup apricot preserves**
- **6 oz thinly sliced roast turkey breast (from deli)**
- **4 to 5 oz Brie cheese, cut into 4 slices**
- **Fresh parsley sprigs, if desired**

1 Heat oven to 375°F. Spray 15x10x1-inch pan with cooking spray. Unroll dough in pan; starting at center, press dough to edges of pan. Bake 7 to 12 minutes or until light golden brown. Cool 5 minutes.

2 Meanwhile, in 10-inch skillet, cook bacon over medium heat, turning once, until crisp. Drain on paper towels.

3 In small bowl, mix mayonnaise and apricot preserves until well mixed. Set aside.

4 Cut pizza crust in half crosswise to make 2 rectangles. Remove rectangles from pan; spread half of the apricot aioli evenly over each rectangle. Top 1 rectangle evenly with turkey, bacon and cheese. Cover with second rectangle, aioli side down. Cut large sandwich in half crosswise; cut each in half diagonally to make 4 sandwiches.

5 Heat 12-inch skillet over medium heat until hot. Place 2 sandwiches in skillet. Place smaller skillet or saucepan on sandwiches to flatten slightly; keep skillet on sandwiches while cooking. Cook 2 to 8 minutes, turning once, until cheese is melted and bread is golden brown. Remove from skillet; cover with foil to keep warm. Repeat with remaining 2 sandwiches. Garnish with parsley.

1 Sandwich: Calories 630; Total Fat 29g (Saturated Fat 10g; Trans Fat 0g); Cholesterol 90mg; Sodium 1360mg; Total Carbohydrate 61g (Dietary Fiber 0g); Protein 32g **Exchanges:** 2½ Starch, 1½ Other Carbohydrate, 3½ High-Fat Meat **Carbohydrate Choices:** 4

spinach-turkey sliders with lemon yogurt sauce

prep time: 35 Minutes • **start to finish:** 35 Minutes • 10 sliders

- **1 can Pillsbury Grands! Jr. Golden Layers Butter Tastin' refrigerated biscuits (10 biscuits)**
- **4 tablespoons olive oil**
- **2 teaspoons sesame seed**
- **1¼ lbs ground turkey**
- **1 box (9 oz) frozen chopped spinach, thawed, squeezed to drain**
- **2 containers (5.3 oz each) fat-free lemon Greek yogurt, stirred**
- **¼ teaspoon garlic powder**
- **1½ teaspoons salt**
- **½ teaspoon pepper**

1 Heat oven to 400°F. Separate dough into 10 biscuits; place 2 inches apart on ungreased cookie sheet. Brush tops of biscuits with 1 teaspoon of the oil. Sprinkle with sesame seed; press in lightly. Bake 8 to 11 minutes or until golden brown.

2 Meanwhile, in large bowl, gently mix turkey, spinach, 2 tablespoons of the yogurt, the garlic powder, 1¼ teaspoons of the salt and ¼ teaspoon of the pepper just until combined. Shape mixture into 10 (3-inch) patties.

3 In 10-inch nonstick skillet, heat 2 tablespoons oil over medium-high heat. Add 5 patties; cook 4 to 6 minutes, turning once, until meat thermometer inserted in center of patties reads 165°F. Drain on paper towel–lined plate. Repeat with remaining patties and remaining oil.

4 In small bowl, mix remaining yogurt, ¼ teaspoon salt and ¼ teaspoon pepper until blended. Split biscuits. Spread 1 tablespoon yogurt sauce over cut side of each biscuit bottom; top with patties. Cover with biscuit tops. Serve with remaining yogurt sauce.

1 Slider: Calories 290; Total Fat 17g (Saturated Fat 4g; Trans Fat 0g); Cholesterol 45mg; Sodium 730mg; Total Carbohydrate 18g (Dietary Fiber 0g); Protein 15g **Exchanges:** 1 Starch, 2 Lean Meat, 2 Fat **Carbohydrate Choices:** 1

grilled pear, brie and caramelized onion sandwiches

prep time: 55 Minutes • **start to finish:** 55 Minutes • 4 sandwiches

- 1 can Pillsbury refrigerated thin pizza crust
- 2 tablespoons olive oil
- 2 cups thinly sliced onions (about 2 large)
- ¼ teaspoon salt
- ¼ teaspoon coarse ground black pepper
- 1 ripe large pear, thinly sliced
- 4 oz Brie cheese, rind removed, thinly sliced

Easy Success Tips

For ease in slicing onions, cut onion in half. Place onion half, cut side down, on cutting board; cut into thin slices.

Caramelized onions can be made ahead of time and refrigerated in a tightly covered container up to 3 days.

When choosing pears, look for firm fruit with no blemishes. To ripen, let stand at room temperature 1 to 2 days.

1 Heat oven to 400°F for dark or nonstick pan (425°F for all other pans). Spray large cookie sheet with cooking spray. Unroll dough on cookie sheet; starting at center, press dough into 15½x11-inch rectangle. Bake 6 minutes.

2 Meanwhile, in 12-inch nonstick skillet, heat 1 tablespoon of the oil over medium heat. Add onions, salt and pepper; cook 6 to 8 minutes, stirring frequently, until onions are golden brown. Remove to plate. Wipe skillet with paper towel.

3 Cut partially baked crust into 8 (5½x4-inch) rectangles. On 4 of the rectangles, evenly spread onion mixture to within ¼ inch of edges. Top evenly with pear and cheese slices. Cover with remaining rectangles. Brush 1½ teaspoons oil over tops of sandwiches.

4 Place 2 sandwiches, oil side down, in same skillet. Brush with ¾ teaspoon oil. Cook over medium heat 4 to 5 minutes or until bottoms are golden brown. Turn; cook 2 to 3 minutes longer or until bottoms are golden brown and cheese is melted. Serve immediately or keep warm. Repeat with remaining 2 sandwiches and remaining ¾ teaspoon oil.

1 Sandwich: Calories 440; Total Fat 21g (Saturated Fat 7g, Trans Fat 0g); Cholesterol 30mg; Sodium 680mg; Total Carbohydrate 51g (Dietary Fiber 3g); Protein 13g
Exchanges: 1½ Starch, 1½ Other Carbohydrate, ½ Vegetable, 1 Medium-Fat Meat, 3 Fat
Carbohydrate Choices: 3½

Make Your Own Grilled Cheese Sandwiches

You just can't go wrong with a grilled cheese sandwich—melty cheese between slices of chewy, crispy bread. Our grilled cheese combinations are full of appetizing flavors to try and all start with refrigerated pizza crust instead of traditional bread. It's a twist worth checking out.

To make one of the sandwiches below, you will need 1 can Pillsbury refrigerated thin pizza crust. All four sandwiches start by prebaking the crust as follows:

Heat the oven to 400°F for dark or nonstick pan (425°F for all other pans). Spray a large cookie sheet with cooking spray. Unroll the dough on cookie sheet; starting at center, press dough into 16x11-inch rectangle. Bake 6 minutes. Cut partially baked crust into 8 (5½x4-inch) rectangles. Heat a 12-inch nonstick skillet over medium heat. Fill sandwiches as directed below.

- **Grilled Cheddar and Bacon Sandwiches** On 4 of the rectangles, evenly arrange thin slices Cheddar cheese, cooked bacon and thin tomato slices. Cover with remaining rectangles. Brush 1½ teaspoons olive oil or butter over tops of sandwiches. Place 2 sandwiches, oil side down, in skillet. Brush with about 1 teaspoon olive oil or butter. Cook over medium heat 4 to 5 minutes or until bottoms are golden brown. Turn; cook 2 to 3 minutes longer or until bottoms are golden brown and cheese is melted. Serve immediately or keep warm. Repeat with remaining 2 sandwiches and olive oil or butter.
- **Grilled Basil-Avocado Sandwiches** On 4 of the rectangles, evenly arrange fresh mozzarella slices, fresh basil leaves, and thin tomato and avocado slices. Or, instead of fresh basil leaves, spread inside of rectangles with basil pesto. Cover with remaining rectangles. Brush 1½ teaspoons olive oil or butter over tops of sandwiches. Place 2 sandwiches, oil side down, in skillet. Brush with about 1 teaspoon olive oil or butter. Cook over medium heat 4 to 5 minutes or until bottoms are golden brown. Turn; cook 2 to 3 minutes longer or until bottoms are golden brown and cheese is melted. Serve immediately or keep warm. Repeat with remaining 2 sandwiches and olive oil or butter.
- **Grilled Gruyère and Ham Sandwiches** On 4 of the rectangles, evenly arrange thin slices Gruyère cheese, ham, and unpeeled apple slices. Cover with remaining rectangles. Brush 1½ teaspoons olive oil or butter over tops of sandwiches. Place 2 sandwiches, oil side down, in skillet. Brush with about 1 teaspoon olive oil or butter. Cook over medium heat 4 to 5 minutes or until bottoms are golden brown. Turn; cook 2 to 3 minutes longer or until bottoms are golden brown and cheese is melted. Serve immediately or keep warm. Repeat with remaining 2 sandwiches and olive oil or butter.
- **Grilled Pepperoni Pizza Sandwiches** On 4 of the rectangles, spread inside of rectangles with marinara sauce. Evenly arrange thin slices provolone cheese and giant slices pepperoni over marinara. Cover with remaining rectangles. Brush 1½ teaspoons olive oil or butter over tops of sandwiches. Place 2 sandwiches, oil side down, in skillet. Brush with about 1 teaspoon olive oil or butter. Cook over medium heat 4 to 5 minutes or until bottoms are golden brown. Turn; cook 2 to 3 minutes longer or until bottoms are golden brown and cheese is melted. Serve immediately or keep warm. Repeat with remaining 2 sandwiches and remaining olive oil or butter. Serve with additional marinara sauce if desired.

Bake-Off® Contest 47, 2014 | **Ann Goncheroski** | Wilkes-Barre, PA

caprese grilled cheese sandwiches

prep time: 30 Minutes • **start to finish:** 30 Minutes • 4 sandwiches

- 1 can Pillsbury refrigerated thin pizza crust
- ½ cup tomato bruschetta with olive oil and basil (from 8-oz jar), drained if necessary
- ¼ cup mascarpone cheese (from 8-oz container)
- 8 oz fresh mozzarella cheese, cut into 8 slices
- 1 tablespoon olive oil
- 1 teaspoon dried basil leaves
- ½ teaspoon garlic sea salt

1 Heat oven to 400°F for dark or nonstick pan (425°F for all other pans). Spray large cookie sheet with cooking spray.

2 Unroll dough on cookie sheet; starting at center, press dough into 16x11-inch rectangle. Bake 6 minutes.

3 Meanwhile, in small bowl, mix bruschetta and mascarpone cheese until well blended.

4 With pizza cutter or sharp knife, cut pizza crust into 4 rows by 2 rows to make 8 (5½x4-inch) rectangles. On each rectangle, spread 1 tablespoon bruschetta mixture to within ¼ inch of edges. On 4 of the rectangles, place 2 slices mozzarella cheese. Top with remaining rectangles, bruschetta side down. Brush 1½ teaspoons of the oil over tops of sandwiches; sprinkle with ½ teaspoon of the basil and ¼ teaspoon of the garlic salt.

5 Heat griddle or 12-inch skillet over medium-low heat (325°F). Place sandwiches, oil side down, on hot griddle. Brush with remaining 1½ teaspoons oil; sprinkle with remaining ½ teaspoon basil and ¼ teaspoon garlic salt. Cook 2 to 3 minutes or until bottoms are golden brown. Turn; cook 2 to 3 minutes longer or until bottoms are golden brown and cheese is melted.

1 Sandwich: Calories 510; Total Fat 31g (Saturated Fat 15g; Trans Fat 0.5g); Cholesterol 70mg; Sodium 760mg; Total Carbohydrate 39g (Dietary Fiber 1g); Protein 19g **Exchanges:** 1½ Starch, 1 Other Carbohydrate, 2 High-Fat Meat, 3 Fat **Carbohydrate Choices:** 2½

stuffed mediterranean sandwiches

prep time: 20 Minutes • **start to finish:** 50 Minutes • 4 sandwiches

- 1 can Pillsbury Grands! Homestyle refrigerated buttermilk biscuits (8 biscuits)
- 1 egg white, slightly beaten
- ½ teaspoon Greek seasoning
- ¾ cup plain hummus (from 8- or 10-oz container)
- 8 oz thinly sliced cooked chicken (from deli)
- 2 cups lightly packed fresh baby kale or baby spinach leaves
- 16 thin slices cucumber
- 2 medium plum (Roma) tomatoes, each cut into 8 slices
- ½ cup crumbled feta cheese (2 oz)

1 Heat oven to 350°F. Spray cookie sheet with cooking spray.

2 Separate dough into 8 biscuits; press each into 5-inch round. Brush tops of 4 rounds with egg white; place rounds, egg white side up, on cookie sheet. Top with remaining 4 rounds; press edges with fork to seal. Sprinkle tops with Greek seasoning.

3 Bake 15 to 19 minutes or until golden brown. Remove from cookie sheet to cooling rack; cool 10 minutes.

4 With serrated knife, cut biscuits in half. Spread hummus evenly over cut sides of biscuits. On biscuit bottoms, layer chicken, kale, cucumber, tomatoes and cheese. Cover with biscuit tops; press down gently.

1 Sandwich: Calories 570; Total Fat 24g (Saturated Fat 9g, Trans Fat 0g); Cholesterol 50mg; Sodium 2160mg; Total Carbohydrate 69g (Dietary Fiber 5g); Protein 20g **Exchanges:** 1 Starch, 3½ Other Carbohydrate, 1 Vegetable, 1½ Very Lean Meat, ½ Medium-Fat Meat, 4 Fat **Carbohydrate Choices:** 4½

Easy Success Tip

Add even more flavor to these sandwiches by using roasted red pepper, roasted garlic or your favorite hummus flavor instead of plain hummus.

open-face greek sandwiches

prep time: 55 Minutes • **start to finish:** 55 Minutes • 8 sandwiches

- 1 can Pillsbury Grands! Homestyle refrigerated buttermilk biscuits (8 biscuits)
- 2 tablespoons olive oil
- 1¼ lbs lean (at least 93%) ground turkey
- ½ cup chopped onion
- ¾ cup tzatziki sauce
- ¼ teaspoon Greek seasoning
- ½ cup julienne-cut sun-dried tomatoes in oil and herbs (from 8.5-oz jar)
- ⅓ cup pitted kalamata olives, coarsely chopped
- 1 cup crumbled feta cheese (4 oz)
- 1 tablespoon chopped fresh oregano leaves

1 Heat oven to 400°F. Separate dough into 8 biscuits; press each into 7x4-inch oval. Brush both sides of dough with 1 tablespoon of the oil. Place 1 inch apart on ungreased cookie sheet. Bake 10 to 12 minutes or until golden brown.

2 Meanwhile, in medium bowl, mix turkey, onion, ¼ cup of the tzatziki sauce and the Greek seasoning until well blended. Shape mixture into 8 (6x3-inch) oval patties; place on cooking parchment paper.

3 In 12-inch nonstick skillet, heat remaining 1 tablespoon oil over medium heat. Add 4 patties to skillet; cook 6 to 8 minutes, turning once, until meat thermometer inserted in center of patties reads 165°F. Remove to plate; cover to keep warm. Repeat with remaining patties.

4 To serve, place turkey burgers on warm biscuits. Spread 1 tablespoon tzatziki sauce on each burger. Top evenly with tomatoes, olives and cheese; sprinkle with oregano.

1 Sandwich: Calories 380; Total Fat 20g (Saturated Fat 7g, Trans Fat 0g); Cholesterol 65mg; Sodium 820mg; Total Carbohydrate 30g (Dietary Fiber 1g); Protein 20g **Exchanges:** 1 Starch, 1 Other Carbohydrate, 2 Very Lean Meat, ½ Medium-Fat Meat, 3 Fat **Carbohydrate Choices:** 2

Easy Success Tips

Tzatziki is a yogurt-cucumber sauce. We used a thick sauce in our testing. Look for it in the dairy section of your grocery store.

For great flavor, check the label on the various brands of Greek seasoning, and look for one that includes several types of dried herbs in addition to salt.

Bake-Off® Contest 39, 2000 | **Beverley Rossell** | Morgantown, IN

italian meatball hoagie braids

prep time: 15 Minutes • **start to finish:** 35 Minutes • 8 sandwiches

- **2 cans Pillsbury refrigerated crescent dinner rolls (8 rolls each) or 2 cans Pillsbury refrigerated Crescent Dough Sheet**
- **16 frozen cooked Italian-style meatballs, 1 to 1½ inch (from 16-oz bag), thawed**
- **1 cup tomato-basil pasta sauce**
- **1 cup shredded mozzarella cheese (4 oz)**
- **1 egg, slightly beaten**
- **¼ cup grated Parmesan cheese**

1 Heat oven to 375°F. Spray 2 cookie sheets with cooking spray.

2 If using crescent rolls: Unroll dough; separate into 8 rectangles. Place rectangles on cookie sheets. Firmly press perforations to seal. If using dough sheets: Unroll dough; cut into 8 rectangles. Place rectangles on cookie sheets.

3 Cut each meatball in half. Place 4 meatball halves lengthwise down center of each rectangle. Top each with 2 tablespoons pasta sauce and 2 tablespoons mozzarella cheese. With scissors or sharp knife, make cuts 1 inch apart on each side of filling. Alternately cross strips over filling.

4 Brush dough with beaten egg; sprinkle with Parmesan cheese. Bake 15 to 20 minutes or until golden brown.

1 Sandwich: Calories 450; Total Fat 25g (Saturated Fat 10g; Trans Fat 3.5g); Cholesterol 95mg; Sodium 1040mg; Total Carbohydrate 35g (Dietary Fiber 1g); Protein 21g **Exchanges:** 2 Starch, ½ Other Carbohydrate, 2 High-Fat Meat, 1½ Fat **Carbohydrate Choices:** 2

roast beef and gorgonzola hoagies

prep time: 40 Minutes • **start to finish:** 40 Minutes • 6 sandwiches

- 2 cans Pillsbury refrigerated crusty French loaf
- ¼ cup vegetable oil
- 2 tablespoons butter
- 1 medium onion, thinly sliced (about 1 cup)
- 1¾ cups beef broth
- ½ lb thinly sliced cooked roast beef (from deli)
- 1 cup mayonnaise or salad dressing
- 2 chipotle chiles in adobo sauce (from 7-oz can), finely chopped
- 1 tablespoon lime juice
- ½ teaspoon pepper
- 1 cup crumbled Gorgonzola cheese (4 oz)

1 Heat oven to 350°F. Spray large cookie sheet with cooking spray. Place loaves of dough, seam side down and 3 inches apart, on cookie sheet. Using sharp knife, cut 4 or 5 diagonal slashes (½ inch deep) on top of each loaf. Bake 22 to 26 minutes or until golden brown.

2 Meanwhile, in 12-inch skillet, heat oil and butter over medium heat. Add onion; cook 15 to 18 minutes, stirring occasionally, until tender. Stir in broth and beef; cook 4 minutes longer. Remove from heat.

3 In small bowl, mix mayonnaise, chiles, lime juice and pepper; set aside.

4 When bread is done baking, set oven control to broil. Cut each loaf in half horizontally, cutting to—but not completely through—one long side; place cut sides up on cookie sheet. Spread ½ cup mayonnaise mixture over cut sides of each loaf. Using slotted spoon, remove beef and onion from broth mixture, reserving broth mixture. Top each loaf with half of the beef and onion; sprinkle with cheese.

5 Broil with tops 6 inches from heat 2 to 3 minutes or until bread is lightly toasted. Cut each sandwich into 3 pieces. If desired, skim fat from reserved broth mixture and serve broth with sandwiches for dipping.

1 Sandwich: Calories 800; Total Fat 50g (Saturated Fat 10g; Trans Fat 0g); Cholesterol 85mg; Sodium 2370mg; Total Carbohydrate 54g (Dietary Fiber 0g); Protein 33g **Exchanges:** 3 Starch, ½ Other Carbohydrate, 3½ Lean Meat, 7½ Fat **Carbohydrate Choices:** 3½

pizza joe crescent sandwiches

prep time: 20 Minutes • **start to finish:** 40 Minutes • 8 sandwiches

- ½ lb ground beef
- ½ cup chopped pepperoni
- ⅓ cup pizza sauce
- 2 cans Pillsbury refrigerated crescent dinner rolls (8 rolls each) or 2 cans Pillsbury refrigerated Crescent Dough Sheet
- 1 cup shredded mozzarella cheese (4 oz)

1 Heat oven to 375°F. In 10-inch nonstick skillet, cook beef over medium-high heat 5 to 7 minutes, stirring occasionally, until thoroughly cooked; drain. Stir in pepperoni and pizza sauce. Heat to boiling, stirring occasionally. Remove from heat.

2 If using crescent rolls: Separate each can of dough into 4 rectangles. Firmly press perforations to seal. If using dough sheets: Cut each sheet of dough into 4 rectangles. Spoon beef mixture onto center of each rectangle; sprinkle each with 1 tablespoon of the cheese. Fold dough over filling; press edges with fork to seal. Sprinkle each with another 1 tablespoon cheese. Place on ungreased cookie sheet.

3 Bake 18 to 20 minutes or until golden brown.

1 Sandwich: Calories 340; Total Fat 20g (Saturated Fat 8g; Trans Fat 0g); Cholesterol 40mg; Sodium 680mg; Total Carbohydrate 25g (Dietary Fiber 0g); Protein 15g **Exchanges:** 1½ Starch, 1½ Medium-Fat Meat, 2½ Fat **Carbohydrate Choices:** 1½

cuban-style sandwich pockets

prep time: 15 Minutes • **start to finish:** 35 Minutes • 6 sandwiches

- 3 tablespoons coarse-grained mustard
- ¼ teaspoon ground cumin
- 2 cans Pillsbury refrigerated Crescent Dough Sheet
- ½ lb ground pork
- 6 slices (¾ oz each) cooked ham (from deli)
- 6 slices (¾ oz each) Swiss cheese
- 18 dill pickle chips

1 Heat oven to 400°F. Spray large cookie sheet with cooking spray.

2 In small bowl, mix mustard and cumin. Unroll dough sheets on work surface. Cut each sheet into thirds. Press each third into 7½x4½-inch rectangle. Spread mustard mixture evenly over each rectangle to within ½ inch of edges.

3 Shape pork into 6 (3-inch) squares; place over mustard on each rectangle. Top each pork patty with 1 slice ham, 1 slice cheese and 3 pickle chips. Fold dough over filling; press edges firmly with fork to seal. Prick top of each pocket 3 times with fork. Place 2 inches apart on cookie sheet.

4 Bake 15 to 18 minutes or until golden brown and meat thermometer inserted in center of pockets reads 160°F.

1 Sandwich: Calories 440; Total Fat 25g (Saturated Fat 11g; Trans Fat 0g); Cholesterol 55mg; Sodium 1460mg; Total Carbohydrate 35g (Dietary Fiber 0g); Protein 20g **Exchanges:** 1 Starch, 1½ Other Carbohydrate, ½ Very Lean Meat, 1 Lean Meat, 1 High-Fat Meat, 2½ Fat **Carbohydrate Choices:** 2

pickled 'n twisted spicy pork cemitas

prep time: 45 Minutes • **start to finish:** 45 Minutes • 6 sandwiches

- 1 can Pillsbury refrigerated original breadsticks
- 36 fresh cilantro leaves
- 1 tablespoon sesame seed
- 1 cup coleslaw mix (from 16-oz bag)
- 5 tablespoons rice vinegar
- 1 tablespoon chopped fresh cilantro
- ⅛ teaspoon salt
- 1 lb bulk mild chorizo sausage
- 6 slices (¾ oz each) Manchego or Mexican melting cheese (quesadilla)

1 Heat oven to 375°F. Line large cookie sheet with cooking parchment paper.

2 Unroll dough on work surface; separate into 12 breadsticks. Pinch ends of 2 breadsticks together to make 1 long breadstick; roll into 18-inch rope. Repeat with remaining dough to make 5 more ropes. Lightly brush breadsticks with water. Place 6 cilantro leaves evenly along each breadstick; gently twist 2 to 3 times into 22-inch rope. Coil each rope into 3-inch spiral shape, tucking ends under and pinching to seal. Place 2 inches apart on cookie sheet. Brush lightly with water; sprinkle with sesame seed.

3 Bake 13 to 19 minutes or until golden brown. Remove from cookie sheet to cooling rack.

4 Meanwhile, in small bowl, toss coleslaw mix, vinegar, chopped cilantro and salt; set aside.

5 Shape sausage into 6 (3½-inch) patties. In 12-inch skillet, cook patties over medium heat 5 to 6 minutes, turning once, until meat thermometer inserted in center of patties reads 160°F. Place 1 cheese slice on each patty. Cover; remove from heat.

6 Drain coleslaw mixture. Cut each roll in half horizontally. On each roll bottom, place 1 patty and 2 rounded tablespoons coleslaw mixture; cover with roll tops.

1 Sandwich: Calories 560; Total Fat 37g (Saturated Fat 15g; Trans Fat 0g); Cholesterol 80mg; Sodium 1480mg; Total Carbohydrate 29g (Dietary Fiber 0g); Protein 28g **Exchanges:** 2 Other Carbohydrate, 4 High-Fat Meat, 1 Fat **Carbohydrate Choices:** 2

potato and sausage crescent burritos

prep time: 25 Minutes • **start to finish:** 1 Hour • 4 burritos

- ½ lb bulk chorizo sausage
- ¼ cup chopped onion
- ¾ cup refrigerated diced potatoes with onion (from 20-oz bag), coarsely chopped
- ½ cup chipotle salsa
- 1 can Pillsbury refrigerated Crescent Dough Sheet
- ½ cup crumbled queso fresco cheese
- 2 tablespoons chopped fresh cilantro
- 1 egg, beaten

1 Heat oven to 350°F. Spray cookie sheet with cooking spray. In 10-inch nonstick skillet, cook sausage and onion over medium-high heat 5 to 7 minutes, stirring occasionally, until sausage is no longer pink; drain. Stir in potatoes and salsa; cook 2 to 3 minutes or until thoroughly heated. Remove from heat. Cool 10 minutes.

2 Meanwhile, unroll dough on work surface or cutting board; starting at center, press into 14x9-inch rectangle. With pizza cutter or sharp knife, cut dough into 4 rectangles.

3 Spoon about ½ cup sausage mixture onto each rectangle to within ½ inch of edges. Sprinkle evenly with cheese and cilantro. Starting with long side, bring up dough over filling and roll up, folding in sides as you roll; pinch seam to seal. Place burritos, seam side down, 2 inches apart on cookie sheet. Brush with egg.

4 Bake 20 to 25 minutes or until golden brown. Cool 10 minutes. Serve with additional salsa if desired.

1 Burrito: Calories 540; Total Fat 34g (Saturated Fat 13g, Trans Fat 0g); Cholesterol 110mg; Sodium 1550mg; Total Carbohydrate 35g (Dietary Fiber 1g); Protein 24g **Exchanges:** 1½ Starch, 1 Other Carbohydrate, ½ Medium-Fat Meat, 2 High-Fat Meat, 3 Fat **Carbohydrate Choices:** 2

Easy Success Tips

For milder burritos, use bulk pork sausage instead of the chorizo sausage.

If queso fresco is not available, substitute shredded mozzarella cheese.

mexican pulled-pork calzones

prep time: 35 Minutes • **start to finish:** 1 Hour • 4 calzones

Cilantro Pesto

- 1½ cups lightly packed fresh cilantro sprigs
- ¾ cup Spanish peanuts
- 2 to 3 cloves garlic, peeled
- 1 jalapeño chile, cut lengthwise in half, seeded
- ⅓ cup olive oil

Filling

- 1 package (15 oz) refrigerated fully cooked pork roast au jus
- 1 cup shredded pepper Jack cheese (4 oz)
- ½ teaspoon ground cumin
- 1 can Pillsbury refrigerated classic pizza crust
- ¼ cup corn salsa (from 16-oz jar)
- 1 teaspoon olive oil

Topping

Sour cream, if desired

1 Heat oven to 400°F for dark or nonstick pan (425°F for all other pans). Spray large cookie sheet with cooking spray.

2 In food processor, place all pesto ingredients. Cover; process about 30 seconds, stopping once to scrape down side with rubber spatula, until well blended. (Pesto will not be totally smooth.) Set aside.

3 Cook pork as directed on package. Remove pork from liquid to small bowl. Shred pork with 2 forks; stir in cheese and cumin until well blended.

4 Unroll dough on work surface; starting at center, press dough into 14x12-inch rectangle. With pizza cutter or knife, cut into 4 (7x6-inch) rectangles. Spread 2 tablespoons pesto over each rectangle to within ½ inch of edges. Spoon pork mixture onto short half of each rectangle; top with corn salsa.

5 Fold and stretch dough over filling; press edges with fork to seal. Place at least 1 inch apart on cookie sheet. Cut 3 slits in top of each calzone. Brush with 1 teaspoon oil.

6 Bake 13 to 16 minutes or until golden brown. Cool 5 minutes; serve with sour cream and remaining pesto.

1 Calzone: Calories 850; Total Fat 50g (Saturated Fat 13g, Trans Fat 0g); Cholesterol 90mg; Sodium 1410mg; Total Carbohydrate 56g (Dietary Fiber 4g); Protein 42g **Exchanges:** 2½ Starch, 1 Other Carbohydrate, 1 Vegetable, 3 Lean Meat, 1½ High-Fat Meat, 5½ Fat **Carbohydrate Choices:** 4

Easy Success Tip

These calzones are as delicious cold as they are hot, and you will probably find yourself using the cilantro pesto recipe over and over. Try these with an ice-cold beer or margarita.

philly cheesesteak calzones

prep time: 20 Minutes • **start to finish:** 45 Minutes • 4 calzones

- 1 tablespoon olive oil
- 2 cups frozen bell pepper and onion stir-fry (from 14.4-oz bag), thawed, drained
- ½ lb thinly sliced cooked roast beef (from deli), coarsely chopped
- 1½ cups shredded smoked or regular provolone cheese (6 oz)
- 1 can Pillsbury refrigerated classic pizza crust
- 1 teaspoon olive oil
- 2 teaspoons grated Parmesan cheese
- 1 teaspoon chopped fresh parsley

Easy Success Tips

Substitute 1 jar (16 ounces) sweet cherry peppers, drained, for the frozen bell pepper and onion stir-fry. Cut a thin slice off the top of each pepper to remove stem and stem base. Scoop out seeds with tip of small spoon; discard. Cut peppers into quarters; continue as directed in step 2.

Serve these calzones with purchased bottled au jus, marinara sauce or your favorite sauce.

1 Heat oven to 400°F for dark or nonstick pan (425°F for all other pans). Spray large cookie sheet with cooking spray.

2 In 10-inch nonstick skillet, heat 1 tablespoon oil over medium-high heat. Pat thawed vegetables with paper towels; add to skillet. Cook about 2 minutes, stirring constantly, until thoroughly heated. Stir in beef. Remove from heat. Stir in provolone cheese; set aside.

3 Unroll dough on work surface; starting at center, press dough into 14x12-inch rectangle. With pizza cutter or knife, cut into 4 (7x6-inch) rectangles. Spread heaping ½ cup beef mixture on half of each rectangle to within ½ inch of edges.

4 Fold and stretch dough over filling; press edges with fork to seal. Place on cookie sheet. Cut 3 slits in top of each calzone. Brush with 1 teaspoon oil. Mix Parmesan cheese and parsley; sprinkle over calzones.

5 Bake 15 to 20 minutes or until golden brown. Cool 5 minutes before serving.

1 Calzone: Calories 520; Total Fat 21g (Saturated Fat 9g, Trans Fat 0g); Cholesterol 60mg; Sodium 1560mg; Total Carbohydrate 52g (Dietary Fiber 3g); Protein 30g **Exchanges:** 2 Starch, 1½ Other Carbohydrate, 2 Very Lean Meat, 1½ High-Fat Meat, 1½ Fat **Carbohydrate Choices:** 3½

ham and cheese sliders

prep time: 20 Minutes • **start to finish:** 50 Minutes • 10 sliders

- 1 can Pillsbury refrigerated crusty French loaf
- 2 tablespoons mayonnaise
- 10 small pieces cooked ham
- 5 thin slices Swiss cheese, cut in half
- 1 cup fresh baby spinach leaves
- 2 tablespoons butter, melted
- 2 teaspoons honey mustard

Easy Success Tips

Use iceberg or romaine lettuce in place of the spinach, or omit the spinach altogether.

Do you have leftover ham? This recipe is a great way to use it.

1 Slider: Calories 400; Total Fat 22g (Saturated Fat 10g; Trans Fat 0g); Cholesterol 60mg; Sodium 880mg; Total Carbohydrate 31g (Dietary Fiber 0g); Protein 20g **Exchanges:** 2 Starch, 1 Lean Meat, 1 High-Fat Meat, 2 Fat **Carbohydrate Choices:** 2

1 Heat oven to 350°F. Spray cookie sheet with cooking spray. Cut loaf of dough crosswise into 10 slices. Place 2 inches apart on cookie sheet. Bake 8 to 10 minutes or until light golden brown. Cool 5 minutes.

2 Cut buns horizontally in half. Spread mayonnaise evenly on cut side of bun bottoms; top each with 1 piece of ham and half piece of cheese. Divide spinach among sandwiches. Cover with bun tops.

3 In small bowl, stir together melted butter and honey mustard. Brush tops of buns with butter mixture.

4 Place sandwiches on large sheet of foil. Bring up 2 sides of foil so edges meet. Seal edges, making tight ½-inch fold; fold again, allowing space for heat circulation. Fold other sides to seal. Place foil packet on cookie sheet.

5 Bake 10 to 12 minutes or until cheese is melted and sandwiches are hot.

mango tango teriyaki sliders

prep time: 30 Minutes • **start to finish:** 30 Minutes • 10 sliders

- 1 cup finely chopped mango
- ¾ cup mayonnaise
- ⅓ cup teriyaki sauce
- 2 teaspoons ground ginger
- 1 teaspoon kosher (coarse) salt
- ½ teaspoon pepper
- 1 can Pillsbury Grands! Jr. Golden Layers refrigerated buttermilk biscuits (10 biscuits)
- 1 lb ground pork
- 2 small avocados, pitted, peeled and thinly sliced

1 Slider: Calories 300; Total Fat 18g (Saturated Fat 5g; Trans Fat 0g); Cholesterol 30mg; Sodium 910mg; Total Carbohydrate 24g (Dietary Fiber 2g); Protein 10g **Exchanges:** 1 Starch, ½ Other Carbohydrate, 1 Lean Meat, 3 Fat **Carbohydrate Choices:** 1½

1 Heat oven to 400°F. In food processor or blender, place ⅔ cup of the mango, the mayonnaise, 1 tablespoon of the teriyaki sauce, 1 teaspoon of the ginger, ½ teaspoon of the salt and ¼ teaspoon of the pepper. Cover; process until smooth. Pour into small bowl; cover and refrigerate.

2 Bake biscuits as directed on can.

3 Meanwhile, in medium bowl, mix pork, remaining ⅓ cup mango, 2 tablespoons teriyaki sauce, and remaining 1 teaspoon ginger, ½ teaspoon salt and ¼ teaspoon pepper just until combined. Shape mixture into 10 patties, about ½ inch thick. Heat 12-inch nonstick skillet over medium-high heat. Add patties; cook 6 to 9 minutes, turning once, until meat thermometer inserted in center of patties reads 165°F. Brush patties with remaining teriyaki sauce.

4 Split biscuits; spread 1 teaspoon mango mayonnaise on split sides of each biscuit. On biscuit bottoms, place avocado and patties. Spread with remaining mango mayonnaise. Cover with biscuit tops.

black bean, corn and quinoa slab pie

prep time: 30 Minutes • **start to finish:** 1 Hour 10 Minutes • 12 servings

- 2 cans Pillsbury refrigerated classic pizza crust
- 1 tablespoon olive oil
- ¼ cup chopped onion
- 3 tablespoons finely chopped seeded jalapeño chiles
- 1 cup chopped orange or red bell pepper
- 1 bag (11.8 oz) frozen honey-roasted sweet corn
- 1 teaspoon ground cumin
- 2 cups cooked quinoa
- 2 cans (15 oz each) black beans, drained, rinsed
- 1 can (19 oz) red enchilada sauce
- 2 cups shredded Mexican cheese blend (8 oz)
- Shredded lettuce and sour cream, if desired

1 Heat oven to 400°F for dark or nonstick pan (425°F for all other pans). Spray 15x10x1-inch pan with cooking spray. Unroll 1 can of dough in pan; starting at center, press dough to edges of pan to form crust. Bake 10 minutes.

2 Meanwhile, in 4-quart saucepan or Dutch oven, heat oil over medium-high heat. Cook onion, chiles, bell pepper, corn and cumin in oil 4 to 5 minutes, stirring frequently, until vegetables are crisp-tender. Remove from heat. Stir in quinoa, beans, 1 cup of the enchilada sauce and 1 cup of the cheese until well mixed. Spoon mixture over partially baked crust.

3 Unroll remaining can of dough; gently stretch or press dough into 15x10-inch rectangle. Lightly fold lengthwise into thirds; carefully place over bean mixture, unfolding and stretching to fit top.

4 Bake 15 to 20 minutes or until golden brown. Sprinkle with remaining 1 cup cheese. Bake 5 to 10 minutes longer or until cheese is melted. Cool 10 minutes. Cut into 12 squares. Top with lettuce, sour cream and remaining enchilada sauce.

1 Serving: Calories 320; Total Fat 9g (Saturated Fat 4g, Trans Fat 0g); Cholesterol 20mg; Sodium 850mg; Total Carbohydrate 44g (Dietary Fiber 7g); Protein 13g **Exchanges:** 1½ Starch, 1½ Other Carbohydrate, ½ Vegetable, 1 Very Lean Meat, 1½ Fat **Carbohydrate Choices:** 3

Easy Success Tip

Quinoa is a tiny, pearl-shaped, ivory-colored grain that expands to four times its size when cooked. It's rich in nutrients, containing more protein than any other grain.

zesty lime fish tacos

prep time: 40 Minutes • **start to finish:** 40 Minutes • 8 tacos

- **1 lb tilapia fillets**
- **½ cup fresh lime juice (2 to 3 limes)**
- **3 cloves garlic, finely chopped**
- **¼ cup all-purpose flour**
- **¼ cup yellow cornmeal**
- **1 can Pillsbury Grands! Homestyle refrigerated buttermilk biscuits (8 biscuits)**
- **6 tablespoons vegetable oil**
- **4½ teaspoons finely chopped chipotle chiles in adobo sauce (from 7-oz can)**
- **½ teaspoon salt**
- **¼ teaspoon pepper**
- **½ cup salsa**
- **½ cup sour cream**
- **1½ cups shredded cabbage**
- **Lime wedges, if desired**

1 Heat oven to 200°F. Cut each fish fillet lengthwise into 4 strips. In shallow glass dish, mix 7 tablespoons of the lime juice and the garlic. Add fish; turn to coat. Let stand while preparing biscuits.

2 On work surface, mix flour and cornmeal. Separate dough into 8 biscuits. Press both sides of each biscuit into flour mixture, then press or roll into 6- to 7-inch round.

3 In 12-inch nonstick skillet, heat 1½ tablespoons of the oil over medium heat. Add 2 biscuit rounds; cook about 1 minute on each side or until golden brown and cooked through. Place on ungreased cookie sheet; keep warm in oven. Cook remaining rounds, adding 1½ tablespoons oil to skillet for each batch. Wipe skillet clean.

4 Heat same skillet over medium-high heat. Add fish and lime juice mixture, chiles, salt and pepper; cook about 5 minutes, turning fish once, until fish flakes easily with fork.

5 In small bowl, mix salsa, sour cream and remaining 1 tablespoon lime juice.

6 Using slotted spoon, divide fish among warm biscuit rounds. Top each with cabbage and 1 to 2 tablespoons salsa mixture. Fold biscuit in half over filling. Serve with any remaining salsa mixture. Garnish with lime wedges.

1 Taco: Calories 400; Total Fat 22g (Saturated Fat 4.5g; Trans Fat 2g); Cholesterol 40mg; Sodium 860mg; Total Carbohydrate 35g (Dietary Fiber 1g); Protein 15g **Exchanges:** 2 Starch, ½ Other Carbohydrate, 1½ Lean Meat, 3 Fat **Carbohydrate Choices:** 2

muffuletta breakfast bagels

prep time: 25 Minutes • **start to finish:** 1 Hour 10 Minutes • 6 bagels

Bagels

- 10 cups water
- ¼ cup honey
- 1 can Pillsbury refrigerated artisan pizza crust with whole grain
- 1 egg white, beaten
- 1 tablespoon water
- 1 tablespoon sesame seed

Scrambled Eggs

- 5 eggs
- ¼ cup water or milk
- ¼ teaspoon salt
- ⅛ teaspoon pepper
- 1 tablespoon butter

Filling

- 6 slices (1 oz each) provolone cheese
- 6 slices (1 oz each) Genoa salami
- 6 tablespoons olive salad (from 12- or 16-oz jar), drained

1 Bagel: Calories 540; Total Fat 30g (Saturated Fat 12g, Trans Fat 0g); Cholesterol 210mg; Sodium 1330mg; Total Carbohydrate 44g (Dietary Fiber 2g); Protein 25g **Exchanges:** 1 Starch, 2 Other Carbohydrate, 1½ Medium-Fat Meat, 1½ High-Fat Meat, 2 Fat **Carbohydrate Choices:** 3

1 Heat oven to 400°F. Line cookie sheet with cooking parchment paper; spray paper with cooking spray. In 4-quart saucepan or Dutch oven, heat 10 cups water and the honey to boiling over medium-high heat. Reduce heat to low.

2 Remove dough from can but do not unroll. Cut dough crosswise into 6 pieces; shape each piece into a ball. Roll each ball into 8-inch rope. Wrap rope around hand, overlapping ends about 1 inch; firmly pinch and roll ends to seal. Gently add 3 bagels to simmering water; cook 1 minute. Using tongs or slotted spoon, turn bagels over; cook 1 minute longer. Place on cooling rack. Repeat with remaining 3 bagels.

3 Place bagels 2 inches apart on cookie sheet. In small bowl, beat egg white and 1 tablespoon water; brush on tops of bagels. Sprinkle with sesame seed. Bake 18 to 22 minutes or until golden brown. Remove from cookie sheet to cooling rack; cool 20 minutes.

4 Meanwhile, in medium bowl, beat eggs, ¼ cup water, the salt and pepper with fork or whisk until well mixed. In 10-inch skillet, melt butter over medium heat. Pour egg mixture into skillet. As mixture begins to set at bottom and side, gently lift cooked portions with pancake turner. Avoid constant stirring. Cook 3 to 4 minutes or until eggs are thickened throughout but still moist.

5 Split bagels; spoon scrambled eggs onto bagel bottoms. Top each with 1 slice cheese, 1 slice salami and 1 tablespoon olive salad. Cover with bagel tops; press gently.

Bake-Off® Contest 41, 2004 | **Renata Stanko** | Lebanon, OR

pb & j waffle sandwiches

prep time: 15 Minutes • **start to finish:** 15 Minutes • 8 servings

- 1 can Pillsbury Grands! Flaky Layers Original refrigerated biscuits (8 biscuits)
- ½ cup peanut butter
- ¼ cup grape jelly
- 1 tablespoon powdered sugar
- 1 cup fresh fruit (such as strawberries, peach slices, grapes)

1 Heat Belgian or regular waffle maker according to manufacturer's directions. Separate dough into 8 biscuits; press or roll each into 4-inch round.

2 Depending on size of waffle maker, place 2 to 4 biscuit rounds at a time in hot waffle maker. Bake 2 minutes or until golden brown. Cool 1 to 2 minutes.

3 Spread peanut butter on 4 of the waffles; spread jelly on remaining 4 waffles. Place jelly-topped waffles on peanut butter-topped waffles. Cut sandwiches in half to serve. Sprinkle with powdered sugar. Garnish with fruit.

1 Serving: Calories 330; Total Fat 16g (Saturated Fat 3.5g; Trans Fat 2g); Cholesterol 0mg; Sodium 620mg; Total Carbohydrate 38g (Dietary Fiber 1g); Protein 7g **Exchanges:** 2 Starch, ½ Other Carbohydrate, 3 Fat **Carbohydrate Choices:** 2½

CHAPTER 3

pizzas

Bake-Off® Contest 47, 2014 | **Tamra Efta** | Princeton, MN

spicy chicken and spinach pizza

prep time: 15 Minutes • **start to finish:** 30 Minutes • 8 servings

- 1 can Pillsbury refrigerated classic pizza crust
- 1 box (9 oz) frozen chopped spinach
- 1 package (6 oz) refrigerated grilled chicken breast strips, cut into bite-size pieces
- 2 tablespoons Sriracha sauce
- ½ cup ranch dressing
- ¼ teaspoon garlic powder
- 1½ cups shredded three-cheese blend (6 oz)

1 Heat oven to 400°F for dark or nonstick pan (425°F for all other pans). Spray large cookie sheet with cooking spray. Unroll dough on cookie sheet; starting at center, press dough into 14x12-inch rectangle. Bake 6 minutes.

2 Meanwhile, microwave frozen spinach as directed on box 3 to 4 minutes to thaw. Drain well; squeeze dry with paper towels.

3 In small bowl, mix chicken and Sriracha sauce. In another small bowl, mix ranch dressing and garlic powder. Spread ranch dressing mixture evenly over partially baked crust. Sprinkle spinach over ranch dressing mixture; top with chicken. Sprinkle with cheese.

4 Bake 8 to 12 minutes or until cheese is melted and crust is golden brown.

1 Serving: Calories 330; Total Fat 17g (Saturated Fat 6g; Trans Fat 0g); Cholesterol 45mg; Sodium 770mg; Total Carbohydrate 27g (Dietary Fiber 1g); Protein 16g **Exchanges:** 1½ Starch, ½ Other Carbohydrate, 1 Very Lean Meat, ½ High-Fat Meat, 2½ Fat **Carbohydrate Choices:** 2

Bake-Off® Contest 46, 2013 | **Anna Zovko** | Tampa, FL

chicken alfredo brunch pizza

prep time: 20 Minutes • **start to finish:** 30 Minutes • 8 servings

- 1 can Pillsbury refrigerated classic pizza crust
- 1 box (9 oz) frozen chopped spinach
- 6 eggs
- 1 tablespoon Alfredo pasta sauce
- 1 tablespoon water
- ½ cup Alfredo pasta sauce
- 2 cups finely chopped cooked chicken breast
- 2 cups shredded mozzarella cheese (8 oz)
- 1 cup French-fried onions (from 2.8-oz can), crumbled

1 Heat oven to 400°F for dark or nonstick pan (425°F for all other pans). Spray 15x10x1-inch pan with cooking spray. Unroll dough in pan; starting at center, press dough to edges of pan. Bake 7 to 9 minutes or until light golden brown.

2 Meanwhile, microwave frozen spinach as directed on box. Drain; squeeze dry with paper towels. Set aside. In medium bowl, beat eggs, 1 tablespoon Alfredo sauce and the water with whisk until well blended. Heat 10-inch nonstick skillet over medium heat. Add egg mixture; cook until set but still moist, stirring occasionally.

3 Spread ½ cup Alfredo sauce over partially baked crust. Top with eggs, chicken, spinach, cheese and onions.

4 Bake 6 to 10 minutes or until crust is golden brown.

1 Serving: Calories 420; Total Fat 21g (Saturated Fat 10g; Trans Fat 0g); Cholesterol 200mg; Sodium 750mg; Total Carbohydrate 30g (Dietary Fiber 1g); Protein 28g **Exchanges:** ½ Starch, 1½ Other Carbohydrate, ½ Vegetable, 1½ Very Lean Meat, 2 Medium-Fat Meat, 2 Fat **Carbohydrate Choices:** 2

sweet-and-spicy chicken flatbread

prep time: 25 Minutes • **start to finish:** 40 Minutes • 6 servings

- 1 large red onion, thinly sliced
- ½ teaspoon salt
- ¼ teaspoon pepper
- ¼ cup water
- 1 can Pillsbury refrigerated thin pizza crust
- 1 cup sweet orange marmalade
- 2 teaspoons Sriracha sauce
- 3 cups chopped deli rotisserie chicken (from 2-lb chicken)
- 1 cup shredded Monterey Jack cheese (4 oz)
- 1 cup firmly packed shredded bok choy

1 Heat oven to 400°F. In 12-inch nonstick skillet, cook onion, salt and pepper over medium heat 5 to 7 minutes, stirring frequently, until onion is softened. Add water; cook and stir until water is evaporated.

2 Unroll dough on dark or nonstick cookie sheet. Bake 6 minutes. Remove from oven; turn crust over.

3 In small bowl, mix marmalade and Sriracha sauce. Spread mixture over partially baked crust to within ½ inch of edges. Top with chicken, cheese and onion.

4 Bake 10 to 12 minutes or until cheese is melted and crust is deep golden brown. Sprinkle with bok choy.

1 Serving: Calories 500; Total Fat 15g (Saturated Fat 6g; Trans Fat 0g); Cholesterol 75mg; Sodium 980mg; Total Carbohydrate 62g (Dietary Fiber 1g); Protein 28g **Exchanges:** 1 Starch, 3 Other Carbohydrate, 1½ Very Lean Meat, 1½ Lean Meat, ½ High-Fat Meat, 1 Fat **Carbohydrate Choices:** 4

roasted poblano chicken pizzettas

prep time: 20 Minutes • **start to finish:** 55 Minutes • 4 pizzas

- 1 medium poblano chile
- 1 box (10 oz) frozen corn and butter sauce, thawed
- 1 cup chopped seeded zucchini
- ½ teaspoon salt
- ¼ teaspoon pepper
- 1 cup refrigerated salsa, drained
- 1 can Pillsbury refrigerated classic pizza crust
- 1½ cups chopped deli rotisserie chicken (from 2-lb chicken)
- 2 cups shredded pepper Jack or Monterey Jack cheese (8 oz)

1 Set oven control to broil. Line broiler pan with foil. Place chile on rack in broiler pan. Broil with top about 5 inches from heat, turning occasionally, until skin is blistered and evenly browned. Wrap chile in foil; let stand 15 to 20 minutes. Peel chile; remove and discard stem, seeds and membranes. Cut into strips; set aside.

2 Heat oven to 400°F for dark or nonstick pan (425°F for all other pans). Spray cookie sheet with cooking spray.

3 In 10-inch nonstick skillet, cook corn and zucchini over medium heat 4 to 5 minutes, stirring frequently, until zucchini is crisp-tender. Stir in chile, salt and pepper; cook 2 minutes, stirring occasionally, until thoroughly heated.

4 In food processor, place salsa. Cover; process until smooth.

5 Unroll dough on cookie sheet. With pizza cutter or knife, cut dough into quarters. Press each quarter to form 8x6-inch oval. Spread 2 rounded tablespoonfuls salsa over each oval; top each with about ⅓ cup chicken, ½ cup corn mixture and ½ cup cheese.

6 Bake 12 to 15 minutes or until crusts are golden brown and cheese is melted. Serve with additional salsa, if desired.

1 Pizza: Calories 630; Total Fat 26g (Saturated Fat 14g; Trans Fat 0.5g); Cholesterol 100mg; Sodium 2050mg; Total Carbohydrate 62g (Dietary Fiber 4g); Protein 37g **Exchanges:** 2½ Starch, 1½ Other Carbohydrate, ½ Vegetable, 2 Very Lean Meat, 2 High-Fat Meat, 1½ Fat **Carbohydrate Choices:** 4

cheesy chorizo breakfast pizza

prep time: 20 Minutes • **start to finish:** 45 Minutes • 8 servings

- 1 can Pillsbury refrigerated classic pizza crust
- 1 bag (11.8 oz) frozen backyard grilled potatoes
- ½ lb bulk chorizo sausage
- 2 cups shredded Mexican cheese blend (8 oz)
- 6 eggs, well beaten
- ⅔ cup crumbled queso fresco cheese
- 2 tablespoons chopped seeded jalapeño chile (1 large)

1 Heat oven to 400°F for dark or nonstick pan (425°F for all other pans). Spray 15x10x1-inch pan with cooking spray. Unroll dough in pan; starting at center, press dough in bottom and up sides of pan. Bake 8 minutes.

2 Meanwhile, microwave potatoes as directed on bag; set aside. In 10-inch skillet, cook sausage over medium-high heat 5 minutes, stirring to break up large pieces, until no longer pink. Drain on paper towels.

3 Spoon sausage over partially baked crust. Top with potatoes and cheese blend. Carefully pour eggs over cheese.

4 Bake 15 to 20 minutes or until edges are golden brown and egg is set. Sprinkle with queso fresco cheese and jalapeño. Let stand 2 to 3 minutes or until queso fresco cheese is slightly melted.

1 Serving: Calories 490; Total Fat 29g (Saturated Fat 13g; Trans Fat 0g); Cholesterol 200mg; Sodium 1140mg; Total Carbohydrate 33g (Dietary Fiber 1g); Protein 25g **Exchanges:** ½ Starch, 1½ Other Carbohydrate, 1½ Medium-Fat Meat, 2 High-Fat Meat, 1 Fat **Carbohydrate Choices:** 2

butternut squash–pesto pizza

prep time: 45 Minutes • **start to finish:** 1 Hour • 8 servings

- 2½ cups diced peeled butternut squash
- ½ cup chopped onion
- 1 tablespoon packed brown sugar
- 1 teaspoon coarse (kosher or sea) salt
- ½ teaspoon pepper
- 2 tablespoons olive oil
- 1 can Pillsbury refrigerated classic pizza crust
- 4 oz pancetta, diced
- 3 tablespoons basil pesto
- ½ cup chopped drained roasted red bell peppers (from a jar)
- ⅓ cup chopped walnuts
- 1 cup shredded Asiago cheese (4 oz)
- ½ cup crumbled feta cheese (2 oz)

1 Heat oven to 400°F. In medium bowl, mix squash, onion, brown sugar, salt, pepper and 1½ tablespoons of the oil. Spread mixture in ungreased 13x9-inch (3-quart) glass baking dish. Bake uncovered about 20 minutes, stirring occasionally, until squash is tender.

2 Grease large dark or nonstick cookie sheet with shortening. Unroll dough on cookie sheet; starting at center, press dough into 13x9-inch rectangle. Bake 7 to 10 minutes or until light golden brown.

3 Meanwhile, in 10-inch skillet, heat remaining ½ tablespoon oil over medium heat. Add pancetta; cook 4 minutes, stirring frequently, until lightly browned. Drain.

4 Spread pesto over partially baked crust. Top with squash mixture, pancetta, roasted peppers, walnuts and cheeses.

5 Bake 6 to 8 minutes or until edges are golden brown. Let stand 5 minutes before cutting.

1 Serving: Calories 360; Total Fat 20g (Saturated Fat 7g; Trans Fat 0g); Cholesterol 30mg; Sodium 1070mg; Total Carbohydrate 33g (Dietary Fiber 2g); Protein 12g **Exchanges:** 2 Starch, 1 High-Fat Meat, 2 Fat **Carbohydrate Choices:** 2

sausage, onion and fennel pizza

prep time: 35 Minutes • **start to finish:** 55 Minutes • 8 servings

- 1 lb bulk pork sausage
- 2 tablespoons olive oil
- 1 cup sliced onion
- 1 cup thinly sliced fennel bulb
- ¼ teaspoon freshly ground pepper
- 1 can Pillsbury refrigerated thin pizza crust
- 1 cup caramelized onion and roasted garlic tomato pasta sauce (from 24-oz jar)
- 2 cups shredded mozzarella cheese (8 oz)
- ½ cup shredded Parmesan cheese (2 oz)
- 1 teaspoon chopped fresh oregano leaves

1 In 12-inch skillet, cook sausage over medium-high heat 6 to 8 minutes, stirring occasionally, until no longer pink; drain. With slotted spoon, remove sausage to bowl; set aside.

2 Add oil to drippings in skillet; add onion and fennel. Cook over medium heat 15 minutes, stirring frequently, until golden brown. Remove from heat. Stir in pepper.

3 Heat oven to 450°F. Spray large cookie sheet with cooking spray. Unroll dough on cookie sheet; starting at center, press dough into 16x13-inch rectangle. Prick crust generously with fork. Bake 5 minutes.

4 Spread pasta sauce over partially baked crust. Top with onion mixture, sausage and cheeses. Bake on lower oven rack 10 to 12 minutes or until cheese is golden brown. Sprinkle with oregano.

1 Serving: Calories 450; Total Fat 29g (Saturated Fat 10g; Trans Fat 0g); Cholesterol 0mg; Sodium 970mg; Total Carbohydrate 26g (Dietary Fiber 2g); Protein 23g **Exchanges:** 1½ Starch, ½ Vegetable, 1 Medium-Fat Meat, 1 High-Fat Meat, 2½ Fat **Carbohydrate Choices:** 1½

spicy sausage and kimchi pizza

prep time: 15 Minutes • **start to finish:** 30 Minutes • 8 servings

- **1 can Pillsbury refrigerated classic pizza crust**
- **½ lb bulk spicy Italian pork sausage**
- **½ cup marinara sauce**
- **1½ cups kimchi (from 14-oz jar), drained, coarsely chopped**
- **¼ cup sliced green onions (4 medium)**
- **2 cups shredded mozzarella cheese (8 oz)**
- **Chopped fresh cilantro, if desired**

1 Heat oven to 400°F for dark or nonstick pan (425°F for all other pans). Spray large cookie sheet with cooking spray.

2 Unroll dough on cookie sheet; starting at center, press dough into 14x12-inch rectangle. Bake 8 minutes or until light golden brown.

3 Meanwhile, in 10-inch nonstick skillet, cook sausage over medium-high heat 8 to 10 minutes, stirring occasionally, until no longer pink; drain.

4 Spread marinara sauce over partially baked crust to within 1 inch of edges. Top with sausage, kimchi, onions and cheese.

5 Bake 10 to 15 minutes or until cheese is melted and crust is golden brown. Sprinkle with cilantro.

1 Serving: Calories 270; Total Fat 11g (Saturated Fat 4.5g, Trans Fat 0g); Cholesterol 25mg; Sodium 820mg; Total Carbohydrate 27g (Dietary Fiber 1g); Protein 14g **Exchanges:** 1 Starch, 1 Other Carbohydrate, 1½ Medium-Fat Meat, ½ Fat **Carbohydrate Choices:** 2

Easy Success Tip

To tone down the heat of this pizza, swap mild Italian sausage for the spicy variety.

Bake-Off® Contest 43, 2008 | **Bee Engelhart** | Bloomfield Hills, MI

spicy double-mozzarella pancetta pizza

prep time: 15 minutes • **start to finish:** 30 minutes • 8 servings

Crust

- 1 tablespoon olive oil
- 2 tablespoons yellow cornmeal
- 1 can Pillsbury refrigerated classic pizza crust

Seasoning Blend

- 2 tablespoons grated Asiago cheese
- 2 tablespoons sesame seed
- 1 teaspoon garlic powder
- 1 teaspoon Italian seasoning
- ½ to 1 teaspoon crushed red pepper flakes

Toppings

- 8 oz fresh mozzarella cheese, cut into ¼-inch cubes
- 2 cups shredded mozzarella cheese (8 oz)
- ¼ cup chopped dry-pack sun-dried tomatoes
- 4 oz thinly sliced pancetta or smoked ham, chopped (about ½ cup)

1 Heat oven to 400°F for dark or nonstick pan (425°F for all other pans). Brush bottom and sides of 15x10x1-inch pan with oil. Sprinkle cornmeal over bottom of pan.

2 Unroll dough in pan; starting at center, press dough to edges of pan. Bake 6 to 8 minutes or until light golden brown.

3 Meanwhile, in small bowl, mix seasoning blend ingredients.

4 Sprinkle toppings in order listed over partially baked crust. Sprinkle seasoning blend over toppings.

5 Bake 7 to 11 minutes or until cheese is melted and crust is golden brown.

1 Serving: Calories 370; Total Fat 18g (Saturated Fat 9g; Trans Fat 0g); Cholesterol 40mg; Sodium 890mg; Total Carbohydrate 29g (Dietary Fiber 0g); Protein 23g **Exchanges:** 1½ Starch, ½ Other Carbohydrate, 2½ Medium-Fat Meat, 1 Fat **Carbohydrate Choices:** 2

QUICK | 6-INGREDIENTS OR LESS

hawaiian ham and pineapple pizza

prep time: 5 Minutes • **start to finish:** 30 Minutes • 6 servings

- 1 can Pillsbury refrigerated classic pizza crust
- 1 can (8 oz) pizza sauce
- 1¾ cups shredded mozzarella cheese (7 oz)
- 1½ cups cubed cooked ham
- ½ cup drained pineapple tidbits in juice (from 8-oz can)

1 Heat oven to 400°F. Unroll dough on ungreased large dark or nonstick cookie sheet; starting at center, press dough into 15x10-inch rectangle. Bake about 8 minutes or until light golden brown.

2 Spread pizza sauce over partially baked crust; top with half of the cheese, the ham, pineapple and remaining cheese.

3 Bake 10 minutes or until crust is deep golden brown and cheese is melted. Cool 5 minutes before cutting.

1 Serving: Calories 350; Total Fat 12g (Saturated Fat 5g; Trans Fat 0g); Cholesterol 40mg; Sodium 1260mg; Total Carbohydrate 38g (Dietary Fiber 2g); Protein 22g **Exchanges:** 1½ Starch, 1 Other Carbohydrate, 1 Lean Meat, 1½ Medium-Fat Meat **Carbohydrate Choices:** 2½

Easy Success Tip

If you are not a fan of pineapple on your pizza, swap out the pineapple for chopped green bell pepper or mushrooms.

sicilian-style pizza with broccoli pesto

prep time: 25 Minutes • **start to finish:** 55 Minutes • 6 servings

- 1 bag (11 oz) frozen Tuscan seasoned broccoli
- 12 oz bulk Italian pork sausage
- 3 tablespoons olive oil
- 2 cans Pillsbury refrigerated crusty French loaf
- ⅓ cup pine nuts
- 12 oz whole milk mozzarella cheese, diced
- 1 large tomato, diced (1½ cups)
- ¼ teaspoon salt
- ¼ teaspoon pepper

1 Heat oven to 400°F. Microwave frozen broccoli as directed on bag. Cut open bag; set aside.

2 Meanwhile, in 10-inch skillet, cook sausage over medium-high heat 5 to 8 minutes, stirring occasionally, until no longer pink; drain.

3 Brush bottom and sides of 15x10x1-inch pan with 2 tablespoons of the oil. Remove dough from cans; cut each loaf lengthwise in half down center to make a total of 4 pieces. Place dough pieces lengthwise in pan; press in bottom of pan to form crust.

4 In food processor, place broccoli and pine nuts. Cover; process until well blended to make pesto. Spread pesto evenly over crust. Top with sausage, cheese and tomato. Sprinkle with salt and pepper; drizzle with remaining 1 tablespoon oil.

5 Bake 25 to 29 minutes or until crust is golden brown and cheese begins to brown.

1 Serving: Calories 740; Total Fat 42g (Saturated Fat 16g; Trans Fat 0g); Cholesterol 75mg; Sodium 1650mg; Total Carbohydrate 58g (Dietary Fiber 3g); Protein 30g **Exchanges:** 1½ Starch, 2 Other Carbohydrate, ½ Vegetable, 1½ Medium-Fat Meat, 2 High-Fat Meat, 3½ Fat **Carbohydrate Choices:** 4

barbecued pork pizza

prep time: 10 Minutes • **start to finish:** 30 Minutes • 6 servings

- 1 can Pillsbury refrigerated classic pizza crust
- 2 cups refrigerated original barbecue sauce with shredded pork (from 18-oz container)
- 2 cups shredded Monterey Jack cheese (8 oz)
- 1 jalapeño chile, thinly sliced
- 1 cup crushed barbecue potato chips
- ¼ cup mayonnaise
- 1 teaspoon Sriracha sauce

1 Heat oven to 400°F. Grease a large dark or nonstick cookie sheet with shortening. Unroll dough on cookie sheet; starting at center, press dough into 15x10-inch rectangle. Bake about 8 minutes or until light golden brown.

2 Spread pork over partially baked crust. Top with cheese and jalapeño.

3 Bake 8 to 10 minutes or until cheese is melted and golden brown. Sprinkle potato chips over pizza.

4 In small bowl, mix mayonnaise and Sriracha sauce until well blended. Spoon into small resealable food-storage plastic bag; cut off small corner of bag. Squeeze bag to drizzle sauce over pizza.

1 Serving: Calories 530; Total Fat 27g (Saturated Fat 10g; Trans Fat 0g); Cholesterol 55mg; Sodium 1170mg; Total Carbohydrate 49g (Dietary Fiber 1g); Protein 24g
Exchanges: 2 Starch, 1½ Other Carbohydrate, 1½ Lean Meat, 1 High-Fat Meat, 2½ Fat
Carbohydrate Choices: 3

Easy Success Tip

Try crushed tortilla chips or French-fried onions instead of the barbecue potato chips on top of this pizza.

loaded baked potato pizza

prep time: 30 Minutes • **start to finish:** 1 Hour • 6 servings

- 1 can Pillsbury refrigerated classic pizza crust
- 1 medium white potato
- 1 tablespoon olive oil
- ¼ teaspoon salt
- ¼ teaspoon pepper
- 1 box (10 oz) frozen broccoli and cheese sauce
- ⅔ cup sour cream
- 1 tablespoon ranch dressing
- 1 cup shredded Colby-Monterey Jack cheese blend (4 oz)
- 5 slices precooked bacon, coarsely chopped
- 1 small tomato, seeded, chopped (½ cup)
- 2 medium green onions, chopped (2 tablespoons)

1 Serving: Calories 410; Total Fat 20g (Saturated Fat 9g; Trans Fat 0g); Cholesterol 45mg; Sodium 1060mg; Total Carbohydrate 42g (Dietary Fiber 2g); Protein 14g **Exchanges:** 2 Starch, 1 Other Carbohydrate, 1 High-Fat Meat, 2 Fat **Carbohydrate Choices:** 3

1 Heat oven to 375°F. Spray large cookie sheet with cooking spray. Unroll dough on cookie sheet; starting at center, press dough into 13x9-inch rectangle. Bake 10 to 13 minutes or until light golden brown.

2 Meanwhile, pierce potato with fork; place on microwavable paper towel. Microwave on High 4 to 5 minutes, turning once, until tender. Cover; let stand 5 minutes. When potato is cool enough to handle, peel and cut into ¼-inch cubes. In medium bowl, mix potato, oil, salt and pepper; set aside.

3 Microwave broccoli as directed on box. Empty from pouch into small bowl to cool slightly; set aside.

4 In another small bowl, mix sour cream and ranch dressing. Spread mixture over partially baked crust to within ½ inch of edges. Sprinkle with ½ cup of the cheese and the bacon. Top with broccoli mixture, potato mixture, tomato, onions and remaining ½ cup cheese.

5 Bake 15 to 22 minutes or until crust is golden brown and cheese is melted. Let stand 5 minutes before cutting.

potato and caramelized onion flatbread

prep time: 35 Minutes • **start to finish:** 1 Hour • 12 servings

- ¾ lb red and purple fingerling or small red potatoes
- 1 can Pillsbury refrigerated artisan pizza crust with whole grain
- 3 tablespoons olive oil
- 3 large onions, thinly sliced (4 cups)
- 1 teaspoon chopped fresh rosemary leaves
- ½ teaspoon salt
- 1 cup shredded fontina cheese (4 oz)
- 1 cup shredded Gruyère cheese (4 oz)
- ¼ cup shredded Parmesan cheese (1 oz)
- Crushed red pepper flakes, if desired

1 Pierce potatoes with tip of sharp knife. Place potatoes in microwavable bowl; add 2 tablespoons water. Cover with microwavable plastic wrap. Microwave on High 4 to 6 minutes or just until tender. Drain; cool. Slice potatoes with serrated knife; set aside.

2 Heat oven to 400°F for dark or nonstick pan (425°F for all other pans). Spray large cookie sheet with cooking spray. Unroll dough on cookie sheet; starting at center, press dough into 14x12-inch rectangle. Brush with 1 tablespoon of the oil. Bake 7 minutes or until light golden brown.

3 Meanwhile, in 10-inch nonstick skillet, heat remaining 2 tablespoons oil over medium-high heat. Cook onions in oil 10 to 14 minutes, stirring frequently, until golden brown. Remove from heat; stir in rosemary and salt.

4 Arrange onions over partially baked crust to within ½ inch of edges. Arrange potato slices over onions. Sprinkle with cheeses and pepper flakes. Bake 15 to 20 minutes or until cheese is melted.

1 Serving: Calories 250; Total Fat 13g (Saturated Fat 5g, Trans Fat 0g); Cholesterol 25mg; Sodium 430mg; Total Carbohydrate 24g (Dietary Fiber 2g); Protein 10g **Exchanges:** 1½ Starch, ½ Medium-Fat Meat, 2 Fat **Carbohydrate Choices:** 1½

Easy Success Tip

When selecting potatoes for this recipe, look for fingerlings that are 1 to 1½ inches in diameter, or red potatoes that are 1½ to 1¾ inches in diameter.

moroccan madness pizzas

prep time: 30 Minutes • **start to finish:** 45 Minutes • 4 pizzas

- 2 tablespoons olive oil
- 3 tablespoons harissa chili paste
- ½ teaspoon salt
- 1 small eggplant, very thinly sliced
- 1 medium zucchini, chopped
- 1 can Pillsbury refrigerated thin pizza crust
- ¾ cup marinara sauce
- 1 clove garlic, finely chopped
- 2 cups shredded mozzarella cheese (8 oz)
- ¼ cup pitted kalamata olives, chopped
- Fresh oregano leaves and chopped fresh mint leaves, if desired

1 Heat oven to 400°F. In medium bowl, beat oil, 1 tablespoon of the chili paste and the salt with whisk until well blended. Add eggplant and zucchini; toss to combine. Place eggplant and zucchini in roasting pan, setting bowl aside for step 3. Roast vegetables uncovered 8 to 10 minutes or until eggplant and zucchini just start to become tender.

2 Grease large dark or nonstick cookie sheet with shortening or cooking spray. Unroll dough on cookie sheet; starting at center, press dough into 15x10-inch rectangle. Cut rectangle into 4 equal pieces; place ½ inch apart on cookie sheet. Tuck corners of each rectangle under and press to make even.

3 In reserved bowl, mix marinara sauce, remaining 2 tablespoons chili paste and the garlic. Spread evenly on dough rectangles. Top with 1½ cups of the cheese, the roasted vegetables and olives. Sprinkle with remaining ½ cup cheese.

4 Bake 10 to 15 minutes or until crust is golden brown and cheese is melted and bubbly. Sprinkle with oregano and mint.

1 Pizza: Calories 550; Total Fat 27g (Saturated Fat 9g; Trans Fat 0g); Cholesterol 30mg; Sodium 1690mg; Total Carbohydrate 54g (Dietary Fiber 6g); Protein 23g **Exchanges:** 1½ Starch, 1½ Other Carbohydrate, 2 Vegetable, 2 Medium-Fat Meat, 3 Fat **Carbohydrate Choices:** 3½

muffin pizza minis

prep time: 15 Minutes • **start to finish:** 30 Minutes • 8 servings

- ½ lb mild Italian sausage links, casings removed and crumbled, or bulk Italian pork sausage
- 1 pouch (9 oz) fire-roasted tomato cooking sauce or 1 cup tomato sauce with garlic, basil and oregano
- 1 can Pillsbury refrigerated classic pizza crust
- ½ cup shredded Italian cheese blend (2 oz)
- Grated Parmesan cheese, if desired

1 Heat oven to 400°F for dark or nonstick pan (425°F for all other pans). Spray 16 regular-size muffin cups with cooking spray.

2 In 10-inch skillet, cook sausage over medium-high heat 5 to 7 minutes, stirring occasionally, until no longer pink; drain. Stir in cooking sauce.

3 Meanwhile, unroll dough on work surface. Cut into 16 equal pieces. Place 1 dough piece in each muffin cup, pressing firmly in bottom and up side near edges. Spoon 1 to 2 tablespoons sausage mixture into each cup; sprinkle evenly with Italian cheese blend.

4 Bake 15 minutes or until edges are deep golden brown. Run knife around edges to remove from muffin cups. Serve with Parmesan cheese.

1 Serving: Calories 220; Total Fat 9g (Saturated Fat 3.5g; Trans Fat 0g); Cholesterol 20mg; Sodium 740mg; Total Carbohydrate 24g (Dietary Fiber 1g); Protein 9g **Exchanges:** 1 Starch, ½ Other Carbohydrate, 1 Lean Meat, 1 Fat **Carbohydrate Choices:** 1½

Easy Success Tips

Muffin cup sizes vary—older varieties tend to be more shallow and hold less, while newer varieties tend to be sized more generously. For this recipe, a more generously sized muffin cup will better accommodate the pizza fillings.

Try substituting mini pepperoni for the Italian sausage, or go meatless and stir some chopped green bell pepper, onion and mushrooms into the cooking sauce.

QUICK | 6-INGREDIENTS OR LESS

buffalo chicken stromboli

prep time: 10 Minutes • **start to finish:** 30 Minutes • 6 servings

- 1 can Pillsbury refrigerated classic pizza crust
- 2 cups shredded cooked chicken
- ¼ cup Buffalo wing sauce
- ⅓ cup crumbled blue cheese

1 Heat oven to 400°F for dark or nonstick pan (425°F for all other pans). Lightly spray cookie sheet with cooking spray. Unroll dough on cookie sheet; starting at center, press dough into 14x10-inch rectangle.

2 In small bowl, mix chicken and Buffalo wing sauce; spread down center of rectangle to within 1 inch of edges. Sprinkle with cheese. Fold shorter sides of dough 1 inch over filling. Bring long sides of dough over filling, overlapping in center; pinch edges to seal.

3 Bake 14 to 16 minutes or until golden brown.

1 Serving: Calories 270; Total Fat 6g (Saturated Fat 2.5g; Trans Fat 0g); Cholesterol 45mg; Sodium 1010mg; Total Carbohydrate 33g (Dietary Fiber 1g); Protein 20g **Exchanges:** 2 Starch, 2 Lean Meat **Carbohydrate Choices:** 2

Easy Success Tip

Buffalo wing sauces vary in flavor. Experiment with different brands to determine your favorite.

Bake-Off® Contest 46, 2013 | **Audrey Lidsky** | Ringwood, NJ

spicy asian shrimp stromboli

prep time: 10 Minutes • **start to finish:** 40 Minutes • 4 servings

- 11 oz frozen panko or breaded shrimp, tail shells removed
- 1 can Pillsbury refrigerated classic pizza crust
- ¼ cup sweet orange marmalade
- ¼ cup hot pepper jelly
- 1 cup finely shredded cabbage
- 2 to 4 tablespoons Sriracha sauce

1 Heat oven to 400°F. Arrange shrimp in single layer on ungreased cookie sheet. Bake 6 minutes.

2 Meanwhile, grease large dark or nonstick cookie sheet with shortening. Unroll dough on cookie sheet; starting at center, press dough into 12x8-inch rectangle.

3 In small bowl, mix marmalade and jelly. Spread over dough to within ½ inch of edges. Place shrimp and cabbage on one side of dough to within ½ inch of edges; drizzle with Sriracha sauce. Fold dough over filling; firmly press edges to seal.

4 Bake 18 to 22 minutes or until deep golden brown. Cool 5 minutes before cutting.

1 Serving: Calories 590; Total Fat 14g (Saturated Fat 3g; Trans Fat 0g); Cholesterol 55mg; Sodium 1400mg; Total Carbohydrate 97g (Dietary Fiber 3g); Protein 18g **Exchanges:** 1½ Starch, 5 Other Carbohydrate, 2 Very Lean Meat, 2½ Fat **Carbohydrate Choices:** 6½

Easy Success Tips

Save time by purchasing a bag of finely shredded cabbage or coleslaw mix instead of slicing a head of cabbage.

pizza cones

prep time: 30 Minutes • **start to finish:** 40 Minutes • 12 pizza cones

- 1 can Pillsbury refrigerated classic pizza crust
- 24 frozen cooked mini meatballs (from 26-oz bag), thawed, cut in half
- 1 jar (14 oz) pizza sauce
- 1 package (3.5 oz) sliced pepperoni
- ¾ cup finely chopped yellow or green bell pepper
- ¾ cup shredded pizza cheese blend (3 oz)

1 Move oven rack to lowest position. Heat oven to 400°F. Wrap 12 (4-oz) cone-shaped paper cups with nonstick foil.

2 Unroll dough on work surface. Using rolling pin, roll dough into 20x15-inch rectangle. Cut into 12 (5-inch) squares. Wrap 1 dough square around each cup; press to seal edges. Trim any excess dough at bottom of cup. Place cones, open end down, on large cookie sheet.

3 Bake on lowest oven rack 8 to 10 minutes or until light golden brown. When cool enough to touch, remove and discard foil-covered paper cups.

4 Place 1 meatball half in bottom of each cone; set aside. In large bowl, mix ¾ cup of the pizza sauce, the pepperoni, bell pepper and remaining meatball halves. Microwave uncovered on High 2 to 4 minutes or until hot. Spoon about ¼ cup of the mixture into each cone. Top each with about 1 tablespoon cheese. Serve hot with remaining pizza sauce.

1 Pizza Cone: Calories 240; Total Fat 11g (Saturated Fat 4.5g; Trans Fat 0g); Cholesterol 45mg; Sodium 630mg; Total Carbohydrate 22g (Dietary Fiber 1g); Protein 12g **Exchanges:** 1½ Starch, 1 Lean Meat, 1½ Fat **Carbohydrate Choices:** 1½

Easy Success Tip

Rather than purchasing paper cups, you can make your own foil cone shapes. Cut 12 (9-inch) rounds of nonstick foil. Fold round in half; starting at one side, roll up foil until bottom open end is 3 inches across. Place each dough square over a foil cone, pressing edges to seal. Reshape foil into cone shape. Bake as directed.

QUICK | 6-INGREDIENTS OR LESS

biscuit sausage calzones

prep time: 10 Minutes • **start to finish:** 25 Minutes • 8 calzones

- 1 can Pillsbury Grands! refrigerated biscuits (8 biscuits)
- ½ cup pizza sauce
- 1 cup crumbled cooked sausage
- 1 cup shredded mozzarella cheese (4 oz)

1 Heat oven to 375°F. Separate dough into 8 biscuits; press each into 5-inch round. Place on ungreased large cookie sheet.

2 Spread 1 tablespoon pizza sauce on half of each round to within ½ inch of edge; top each with 2 tablespoons each of the sausage and cheese. Fold dough over filling; press edges with fork to seal.

3 Bake 12 to 15 minutes or until golden brown.

1 Calzone: Calories 280; Total Fat 15g (Saturated Fat 5g; Trans Fat 3.5g); Cholesterol 20mg; Sodium 810mg; Total Carbohydrate 27g (Dietary Fiber 0g); Protein 10g
Exchanges: 1 Starch, 1 Other Carbohydrate, ½ Lean Meat, ½ Medium-Fat Meat, 2 Fat
Carbohydrate Choices: 2

Easy Success Tip

Use leftover sausage in these calzones, or look for precooked sausage in the refrigerated section of your supermarket.

two-cheese calzones

prep time: 20 Minutes • **start to finish:** 45 Minutes • 6 calzones

- 1 can Pillsbury refrigerated thin pizza crust
- ¼ cup ricotta cheese
- 4 sticks (1 oz each) string cheese, diced
- 1½ cups marinara sauce

1 Heat oven to 400°F for dark or nonstick pan (425°F for all other pans). Lightly spray cookie sheet with cooking spray.

2 Unroll dough on cookie sheet; starting at center, press dough into 15x10-inch rectangle. Cut into 6 (5-inch) squares. Spread 2 teaspoons ricotta cheese on half of each square to within ½ inch of edges; top each with 2 tablespoons diced cheese sticks and 1 tablespoon marinara sauce. Fold dough in half over filling; press edges firmly with fork to seal.

3 Bake about 15 minutes or until golden brown. Cool 10 minutes. Meanwhile, in 1-quart saucepan, heat remaining marinara sauce over medium heat until warm. Serve with calzones.

1 Calzone: Calories 290; Total Fat 11g (Saturated Fat 3.5g; Trans Fat 0g); Cholesterol 15mg; Sodium 740mg; Total Carbohydrate 37g (Dietary Fiber 2g); Protein 11g **Exchanges:** 2½ Starch, ½ Medium-Fat Meat, 1½ Fat **Carbohydrate Choices:** 2½

Grilled Pizza — Two Easy Methods

It's easy to cook restaurant-style grilled pizza at home on your own grill. Whether you grill year-round or want to take the heat out of the kitchen during the summer months, we offer two methods and five tasty new recipes. In both methods, the crust is briefly cooked without toppings so it sets up and browns a bit. This ensures that it will cook all the way through since pizza cooks so quickly on the grill. It also helps the crust to stay crisp. Pair the pizza with your favorite beverages plus a salad and enjoy!

Pizza Cooked Directly on the Grill Rack

Add extra smokiness and crispiness to the crust by cooking it directly on the grill rack from start to finish. Once you've mastered this easy technique, all of your friends will want to come to your house for great-tasting pizza. Try Grilled Sausage and Pepper Pizza, page 159, or Grilled Spinach and Mushroom Pizza, page 162.

- Make sure the grill rack is clean before you start grilling so the crust doesn't stick.
- Use a long-handled, wide spatula for handling the crust and removing the pizza from the grill rack. Have a serving platter or cookie sheet right next to the grill to put the hot pizza on.

Pizza Cooked on Foil on the Grill Rack

Grilling the pizza from start to finish on foil on the grill rack is an easy, no-fuss method. The foil still allows the pizza to cook quickly and the bottom to crisp. And of course, clean-up is as easy as removing the pizza from the grill. Try Spicy Grilled Thai Pizza, page 158, Easy Grilled Nacho Pizza, page 160, and Grilled Fresh Veggie Pizza, page 164.

- Heavy-duty foil is the thickest and works great on the grill. If you don't have it, just double-up a sheet of regular foil.

spicy grilled thai pizza

prep time: 25 Minutes • **start to finish:** 25 Minutes • 4 servings

- 1 can Pillsbury refrigerated thin pizza crust
- ¼ cup peanut sauce
- 1 cup chopped cooked chicken breast
- ½ cup shredded carrot
- 2 medium green onions, chopped (2 tablespoons)
- 2 tablespoons coarsely chopped peanuts
- ⅓ cup finely shredded mozzarella cheese
- 2 tablespoons chopped fresh cilantro

1 Heat gas or charcoal grill. Cut 14x14-inch sheet of heavy-duty foil; spray foil with cooking spray. Unroll dough on foil; starting at center, press dough into 12-inch round.

2 Place dough, foil side down, on grill over medium heat. Cover grill; cook 3 minutes or until bottom of crust is light golden brown. Remove from grill.

3 Using wide spatula, flip crust over onto foil so uncooked side is down. Spread peanut sauce over crust. Top with chicken, carrot, onions and peanuts. Sprinkle with cheese.

4 Leaving pizza on foil, place pizza on grill. Cover grill; cook 3 to 4 minutes or until crust is golden brown and cheese begins to melt. Sprinkle with cilantro.

1 Serving: Calories 390; Total Fat 16g (Saturated Fat 4g; Trans Fat 0g); Cholesterol 35mg; Sodium 570mg; Total Carbohydrate 41g (Dietary Fiber 2g); Protein 22g **Exchanges:** 2 Starch, ½ Other Carbohydrate, 2½ Lean Meat, 1½ Fat **Carbohydrate Choices:** 3

Easy Success Tip

To make a barbecue-flavored chicken pizza, substitute barbecue sauce for the peanut sauce. Omit the carrot and chopped peanuts. Use Cheddar cheese instead of mozzarella.

grilled sausage and pepper pizza

prep time: 45 Minutes • **start to finish:** 45 Minutes • 6 servings

- 3 links hot Italian turkey sausage (from 19.5-oz package)
- 1 can Pillsbury refrigerated artisan pizza crust with whole grain or Pillsbury refrigerated classic pizza crust
- Cooking spray
- ¾ cup pizza sauce
- 1 cup torn fresh basil leaves
- 2 cups shredded reduced-fat mozzarella cheese (8 oz)
- 1 large red bell pepper, thinly sliced, cut into bite-size pieces (1 cup)

1 Serving: Calories 410; Total Fat 18g (Saturated Fat 7g; Trans Fat 0g); Cholesterol 50mg; Sodium 1010mg; Total Carbohydrate 37g (Dietary Fiber 3g); Protein 25g **Exchanges:** 2 Starch, ½ Other Carbohydrate, ½ Vegetable, 1½ Lean Meat, 1 Medium-Fat Meat, 1½ Fat **Carbohydrate Choices:** 2½

Easy Success Tip

Have all the toppings ready to go—the crust cooks quickly. If the crust is cooking too fast, move the pizza to a cooler part of the grill, or reduce the heat.

1 Heat gas or charcoal grill. Place sausages on grill over medium heat. Cover grill; cook 18 to 20 minutes, turning occasionally, until no longer pink in center. Cool 5 minutes. Cut sausages at an angle into ¼-inch slices; set aside.

2 Cut 18x12-inch sheet of heavy-duty foil; place on large cookie sheet. Spray foil with cooking spray. Unroll dough on foil; starting at center, press dough into 14x10-inch rectangle. Spray dough with cooking spray.

3 Invert dough directly onto grill rack; peel off foil and return foil to cookie sheet, sprayed side up. Cook uncovered over medium-low heat 2 to 4 minutes or until bottom is golden brown. (Watch carefully to prevent burning.) With wide spatula, turn crust over. Cook 1 to 2 minutes longer or until bottom is set but not browned. Carefully remove from grill; place crust, browned side up, on foil.

4 Spread pizza sauce over crust; top with basil, 1¾ cups of the cheese, the sausage and bell pepper. Sprinkle with remaining ¼ cup cheese. Slide pizza from foil onto grill. Cover grill; cook 3 to 5 minutes or until crust is golden brown and cheese is melted.

easy grilled nacho pizza

prep time: 25 Minutes • **start to finish:** 25 Minutes • 4 servings

- 1 can Pillsbury refrigerated thin pizza crust
- ¼ cup spicy bean dip
- 1 cup refrigerated taco sauce with seasoned ground beef (from 18-oz container)
- 1 can (4.5 oz) chopped green chiles
- 1 medium tomato, chopped (½ cup)
- ¼ cup sliced green onions (4 medium)
- 1 cup finely shredded Cheddar cheese (4 oz)
- Guacamole and sour cream, if desired

1 Heat gas or charcoal grill. Cut 14x14-inch sheet of heavy-duty foil; spray foil with cooking spray. Place dough on foil; starting at center, press dough into 12-inch round.

2 Place dough, foil side down, on grill over medium heat. Cook uncovered 3 minutes or until bottom of crust is light golden brown. Remove from grill.

3 Using wide spatula, flip crust over onto foil so uncooked side is down. Spread bean dip over crust; spoon beef mixture evenly over dip. Sprinkle with chiles, tomato, onions and cheese.

4 Leaving pizza on foil, place pizza on grill. Cover; cook 3 to 4 minutes or until crust is golden brown and cheese begins to melt. Serve with guacamole and sour cream.

1 Serving: Calories 470; Total Fat 23g (Saturated Fat 10g; Trans Fat 1g); Cholesterol 50mg; Sodium 1180mg; Total Carbohydrate 46g (Dietary Fiber 2g); Protein 19g **Exchanges:** 3 Starch, ½ Vegetable, ½ Medium-Fat Meat, 1 High-Fat Meat, 2 Fat **Carbohydrate Choices:** 3

grilled spinach and mushroom pizza

prep time: 25 Minutes • **start to finish:** 25 Minutes • 4 servings

- **1 can Pillsbury refrigerated thin pizza crust**
- **Cooking spray**
- **1 can (8 oz) pizza sauce**
- **2 cups torn fresh baby spinach leaves**
- **1 cup sliced fresh mushrooms (3 oz)**
- **1 cup shredded mozzarella cheese (4 oz)**

1 Heat gas or charcoal grill. Cut 18x12-inch sheet of heavy-duty foil; place on large cookie sheet. Spray foil with cooking spray. Unroll dough on foil; starting at center, press dough into 14x10-inch rectangle. Spray dough with cooking spray.

2 Invert dough rectangle directly onto grill rack; peel off foil and return foil to cookie sheet, sprayed side up. Cook uncovered over medium-low heat 2 to 4 minutes or until bottom is golden brown. (Watch carefully to prevent burning.) With wide spatula, turn crust over. Cook 1 to 2 minutes longer or until bottom is set but not browned. Carefully remove from grill; place crust, browned side up, on foil.

3 Spread pizza sauce over crust; top with spinach and mushrooms. Sprinkle with cheese. Slide pizza from foil onto grill. Cover grill; cook 3 to 6 minutes or until crust is golden brown and cheese is melted.

1 Serving: Calories 360; Total Fat 13g (Saturated Fat 5g; Trans Fat 0g); Cholesterol 15mg; Sodium 720mg; Total Carbohydrate 43g (Dietary Fiber 3g); Protein 15g **Exchanges:** 2 Starch, ½ Other Carbohydrate, 1½ Vegetable, 1 Lean Meat, 2 Fat **Carbohydrate Choices:** 3

Easy Success Tips

Have all the toppings ready to go because the crust cooks quickly. If the crust is cooking too fast, move the pizza to a cooler part of the grill or reduce the heat.

If you are not grilling, you can bake the pizza in the oven by following the directions on the can that use a prebake time.

grilled fresh veggie pizza

prep time: 30 Minutes • **start to finish:** 30 Minutes • 8 servings

- 1½ cups thinly sliced red or yellow bell peppers or ¾ cup of each
- 1 cup thinly sliced sweet onion
- 1 cup sliced fresh baby portabella mushrooms (3 oz)
- 1 cup sliced zucchini
- ¼ cup French vinaigrette or Italian dressing
- 1 can Pillsbury refrigerated thin pizza crust
- 1 container (6.5 oz) savory gourmet spreadable cheese with savory vegetables
- 1 cup finely shredded mozzarella cheese (4 oz)
- ¾ cup quartered grape or cherry tomatoes

1 Heat gas or charcoal grill. In large bowl, toss bell peppers, onion, mushrooms, zucchini and vinaigrette to coat.

2 Place vegetables in grill basket (grill "wok"). Place basket on grill over medium-high heat. Cook 8 to 12 minutes, stirring once or twice, until vegetables are tender. Remove from grill; set aside.

3 Cut 14x14-inch sheet of heavy-duty foil; spray foil with cooking spray. Place dough on foil; starting at center, press dough into 12-inch round. Place dough, foil side down, on grill. Cook uncovered 3 minutes or until bottom of crust is light golden brown. Remove from grill.

4 Using wide spatula, flip crust over onto foil so uncooked side is down. Spread gourmet cheese over crust; top with grilled vegetables. Sprinkle with mozzarella cheese and tomatoes.

5 Leaving pizza on foil, place pizza on grill. Cover grill; cook 3 to 4 minutes or until crust is golden brown and cheese is melted.

1 Serving: Calories 280; Total Fat 16g (Saturated Fat 7g; Trans Fat 0g); Cholesterol 30mg; Sodium 510mg; Total Carbohydrate 25g (Dietary Fiber 1g); Protein 9g **Exchanges:** 1½ Starch, 1 Vegetable, ½ Medium-Fat Meat, 2½ Fat **Carbohydrate Choices:** 1½

CHAPTER 4

casseroles and savory pies

turkey and stuffing crescent bake

prep time: 10 Minutes • **start to finish:** 35 Minutes • 6 servings

- 2 cups prepared stuffing
- 1½ cups cubed cooked turkey
- ½ cup turkey gravy
- 1 can Pillsbury refrigerated Crescent Dough Sheet or 1 can Pillsbury refrigerated crescent dinner rolls (8 rolls)
- 1 cup cranberry sauce

1 Heat oven to 375°F. In 2-quart saucepan, mix stuffing, turkey and gravy. Heat to boiling over medium-high heat, stirring occasionally. Spoon into ungreased 8-inch square (2-quart) glass baking dish.

2 If using dough sheet: Unroll dough; cut into 4 rectangles. If using crescent rolls: Unroll dough; separate into 4 rectangles. Firmly press perforations to seal. Place rectangles over stuffing mixture, leaving space between rectangles for steam to escape.

3 Bake 20 to 25 minutes or until crust is golden brown. Serve with cranberry sauce.

1 Serving: Calories 430; Total Fat 17g (Saturated Fat 5g; Trans Fat 2.5g); Cholesterol 45mg; Sodium 740mg; Total Carbohydrate 49g (Dietary Fiber 1g); Protein 19g **Exchanges:** 2 Starch, 1½ Other Carbohydrate, 2 Lean Meat, 2 Fat **Carbohydrate Choices:** 3

QUICK | 6-INGREDIENTS OR LESS

chicken-chili crescent bake

prep time: 10 Minutes • **start to finish:** 30 Minutes • 8 servings

- 3 cups shredded cooked chicken
- 1 can (15 oz) cannellini beans, drained
- 1 can (10 oz) diced tomatoes with green chiles
- 2 tablespoons taco seasoning mix (from 1-oz package)
- 1 can Pillsbury refrigerated crescent dinner rolls (8 rolls)

1 Heat oven to 375°F. In 3-quart saucepan, mix chicken, beans, tomatoes and taco seasoning mix. Heat over medium-high heat, stirring occasionally, until hot. Spoon into ungreased 13x9-inch (3-quart) glass baking dish.

2 Separate dough into 8 triangles; arrange on top of hot chicken mixture.

3 Bake 18 to 25 minutes.

1 Serving: Calories 270; Total Fat 10g (Saturated Fat 3g; Trans Fat 1.5g); Cholesterol 45mg; Sodium 900mg; Total Carbohydrate 24g (Dietary Fiber 3g); Protein 20g **Exchanges:** 1½ Starch, 1 Very Lean Meat, 1 Lean Meat, 1 Fat **Carbohydrate Choices:** 1½

chicken and white bean bruschetta bake

prep time: 15 Minutes • **start to finish:** 45 Minutes • 4 servings (1½ cups each)

- 1 can (19 oz) cannellini (white kidney) beans, drained, rinsed
- 1 can (14.5 oz) organic diced tomatoes with Italian herbs, drained
- 1 package (6 oz) refrigerated cooked Italian-style chicken breast strips, cut into 1-inch pieces
- 1 tablespoon balsamic vinegar
- ½ teaspoon salt
- 1 can Pillsbury refrigerated original breadsticks
- 2 cups shredded 6-cheese Italian cheese blend (8 oz)
- ½ teaspoon dried basil leaves, crushed
- 1 tablespoon chopped fresh parsley, if desired

1 Heat oven to 375°F. Spray 13x9-inch (3-quart) glass baking dish with cooking spray. In large bowl, mix beans, tomatoes, chicken, vinegar and salt.

2 Unroll dough; separate into 12 breadsticks. Cut each breadstick into 4 equal pieces. Stir ¼ of breadstick pieces at a time into bean mixture. Stir in 1 cup of the cheese. Spoon into baking dish, gently smoothing top. Top evenly with remaining 1 cup cheese; sprinkle with basil.

3 Bake 25 to 30 minutes or until bubbly and top is golden brown. To serve, spoon into individual shallow soup bowls; sprinkle with parsley.

1 Serving: Calories 630; Total Fat 20g (Saturated Fat 10g; Trans Fat 1g); Cholesterol 80mg; Sodium 1880mg; Total Carbohydrate 73g (Dietary Fiber 8g); Protein 40g **Exchanges:** 3½ Starch, 1 Other Carbohydrate, 1 Vegetable, 4 Very Lean Meat, 3 Fat **Carbohydrate Choices:** 5

mexi-beef casserole

prep time: 20 Minutes • **start to finish:** 45 Minutes • 5 servings

- **1 lb lean (at least 80%) ground beef**
- **¼ cup chopped onion**
- **2 tablespoons taco seasoning mix (from 1-oz package)**
- **1 can (11 oz) whole kernel corn with red and green peppers, drained**
- **2 cans (8 oz each) tomato sauce**
- **4 oz Cheddar cheese, cut into ½-inch cubes (1 cup)**
- **1 can Pillsbury Grands! Jr. Golden Homestyle refrigerated buttermilk biscuits (10 biscuits)**
- **1 tablespoon butter, melted**
- **1 teaspoon yellow cornmeal, if desired**

1 Heat oven to 375°F. In 10-inch ovenproof skillet, cook beef and onion over medium-high heat 5 to 7 minutes, stirring occasionally, until beef is thoroughly cooked; drain. Reduce heat to medium; stir in taco seasoning mix, corn and tomato sauce. Heat until hot. Stir in cheese.

2 Separate dough into 10 biscuits; cut each biscuit into quarters. Arrange biscuit pieces around outer edge of skillet. Brush biscuits with butter; sprinkle with cornmeal.

3 Bake 18 to 22 minutes or until biscuits are golden brown.

1 Serving: Calories 470; Total Fat 22g (Saturated Fat 10g; Trans Fat 1g); Cholesterol 85mg; Sodium 1590mg; Total Carbohydrate 41g (Dietary Fiber 3g); Protein 27g **Exchanges:** 2 Starch, ½ Other Carbohydrate, 1 Vegetable, 2½ Medium-Fat Meat, 1½ Fat **Carbohydrate Choices:** 3

Easy Success Tip

Be sure that the skillet you use for this easy meal can go in the oven, handle and all.

sloppy joe casserole

prep time: 15 Minutes • **start to finish:** 30 Minutes • 6 servings

- 1 lb lean (at least 80%) ground beef
- 1 can (15.5 or 16 oz) sloppy joe sauce
- 1 can Pillsbury refrigerated original breadsticks
- ½ cup shredded Cheddar cheese (2 oz)

Easy Success Tip

Taste the sloppy joe sauce before you use it in this casserole; sweeten it with about 1 tablespoon of brown sugar, if desired.

1 Heat oven to 375°F. In 12-inch nonstick skillet, cook beef over medium-high heat 5 to 7 minutes, stirring occasionally, until thoroughly cooked; drain. Stir in sloppy joe sauce. Heat to boiling, stirring occasionally.

2 Meanwhile, separate dough into 12 breadsticks. Cut each into 4 pieces. Pour beef mixture into ungreased 12x8-inch or 11x7-inch (2-quart) glass baking dish. Arrange dough pieces in single layer over beef mixture.

3 Bake 13 minutes. Sprinkle with cheese; bake about 2 minutes longer or until cheese is melted.

1 Serving: Calories 340; Total Fat 14g (Saturated Fat 7g; Trans Fat 0.5g); Cholesterol 55mg; Sodium 900mg; Total Carbohydrate 32g (Dietary Fiber 1g); Protein 20g **Exchanges:** 1½ Starch, ½ Other Carbohydrate, 2 Medium-Fat Meat, ½ Fat **Carbohydrate Choices:** 2

zesty italian crescent casserole

prep time: 20 Minutes • **start to finish:** 45 Minutes • 6 servings

- 1 lb lean (at least 80%) ground beef
- ¼ cup chopped onion
- 1 cup tomato pasta sauce
- 1½ cups shredded mozzarella or Monterey Jack cheese (6 oz)
- ½ cup sour cream
- 1 can Pillsbury refrigerated crescent dinner rolls (8 rolls)
- ⅓ cup grated Parmesan cheese
- 2 tablespoons butter or margarine, melted

Easy Success Tip

The casserole can be baked in an 11x7-inch (2-quart) glass baking dish instead of a pie plate. Separate dough into 4 rectangles, pressing perforations to seal. Arrange rectangles over cheese mixture.

1 Heat oven to 375°F. In 10-inch skillet, cook beef and onion over medium-high heat 5 to 7 minutes, stirring occasionally, until beef is thoroughly cooked; drain. Stir in pasta sauce; cook until thoroughly heated.

2 Meanwhile, in medium bowl, mix mozzarella cheese and sour cream. Pour hot beef mixture into ungreased 9½- or 10-inch glass deep-dish pie plate. Spoon cheese mixture over beef mixture.

3 Separate dough into 8 triangles. Arrange triangles, points toward center, over cheese mixture; seal dough to edge of plate. In small bowl, mix Parmesan cheese and butter. Spread over dough.

4 Bake 18 to 25 minutes or until crust is deep golden brown.

1 Serving: Calories 480; Total Fat 31g (Saturated Fat 15g, Trans Fat 1g); Cholesterol 85mg; Sodium 800mg; Total Carbohydrate 23g (Dietary Fiber 0g); Protein 26g **Exchanges:** 1 Starch, ½ Other Carbohydrate, 2 Lean Meat, 1 Medium-Fat Meat, 4 Fat **Carbohydrate Choices:** 1½

cheesy biscuit, bean and beef casserole

prep time: 15 Minutes • **start to finish:** 35 Minutes • 6 servings

- ½ **lb lean (at least 80%) ground beef**
- ½ **cup chopped onion**
- 1 **can (21 oz) baked beans with bacon and brown sugar sauce, undrained**
- 1 **can (16 oz) kidney beans, drained, rinsed**
- 1 **can (15.8 oz) great northern beans, drained, rinsed**
- ½ **cup barbecue sauce**
- 1 **can Pillsbury Grands! Homestyle refrigerated buttermilk biscuits, separated and each cut into 6 pieces (5 biscuits)**
- ½ **cup finely shredded Cheddar cheese (2 oz)**

1 Heat oven to 350°F. Spray 11x7-inch (2-quart) glass baking dish with cooking spray.

2 In 12-inch nonstick skillet, cook beef and onion over medium heat 4 to 6 minutes, stirring occasionally, until beef is thoroughly cooked; drain. Stir in baked beans, kidney beans, great northern beans and barbecue sauce. Heat to boiling, stirring occasionally. Pour into baking dish. Immediately top hot mixture with biscuit pieces. Sprinkle with cheese.

3 Bake 18 to 20 minutes or until biscuits are golden brown and baked through.

1 Serving: Calories 700; Total Fat 20g (Saturated Fat 8g; Trans Fat 3g); Cholesterol 45mg; Sodium 1490mg; Total Carbohydrate 96g (Dietary Fiber 14g); Protein 34g **Exchanges:** 4 Starch, 3 Vegetable, 3 Lean Meat, 2½ Fat **Carbohydrate Choices:** 6½

beef stew casserole

prep time: 20 Minutes • **start to finish:** 1 Hour 10 Minutes • 6 servings

- 2 tablespoons olive or vegetable oil
- 1 lb boneless beef round steak (½ inch thick), cut into 1-inch pieces
- ½ teaspoon dried thyme leaves
- ⅛ teaspoon pepper
- 2 cups frozen mixed vegetables (from 12-oz bag)
- 2 cups refrigerated cooked diced potatoes with onions (from 20-oz bag)
- 1 can (14.5 oz) diced tomatoes with roasted garlic and onion, undrained
- 1 jar (12 oz) beef gravy
- 1 jar (4.5 oz) sliced mushrooms, drained
- 1 can Pillsbury Grands! Jr. Golden Layers refrigerated buttermilk biscuits (10 biscuits)
- Chopped fresh parsley, if desired

1 Heat oven to 375°F. In 10-inch skillet, heat oil over medium-high heat. Add beef; sprinkle with thyme and pepper. Cook 5 to 7 minutes, stirring occasionally, until browned.

2 Meanwhile, in large bowl, mix vegetables, potatoes, tomatoes, gravy and mushrooms. Stir in beef. Pour mixture into ungreased 13x9-inch (3-quart) glass baking dish.

3 Cover with foil. Bake 28 to 30 minutes or until bubbly around edges.

4 Separate dough into 10 biscuits; cut each biscuit into quarters. Arrange biscuit pieces on beef mixture, leaving space between pieces.

5 Bake uncovered 14 to 18 minutes or until biscuits are golden brown. Sprinkle with parsley.

1 Serving: Calories 440; Total Fat 16g (Saturated Fat 4g; Trans Fat 2.5g); Cholesterol 45mg; Sodium 1210mg; Total Carbohydrate 47g (Dietary Fiber 5g); Protein 26g
Exchanges: 2 Starch, 1 Other Carbohydrate, 1 Vegetable, 2½ Lean Meat, 1½ Fat
Carbohydrate Choices: 3

Easy Success Tip

Lean beef stew meat can be substituted for the round steak.

biscuit-topped thai pork stew

prep time: 45 Minutes • **start to finish:** 1 Hour 10 Minutes • 5 servings

- ⅓ cup all-purpose flour
- ½ teaspoon garlic-pepper blend
- 1½ lbs boneless pork loin chops, cut into 1-inch cubes
- 3 tablespoons olive oil
- 2 cups cubed peeled butternut squash (about 9 oz)
- 1 bottle (11.5 oz) Thai peanut sauce
- 1 cup chicken broth
- ½ teaspoon crushed red pepper flakes
- 1 medium red bell pepper, cut into 1-inch pieces
- 4 oz fresh sugar snap peas, cut diagonally in half (about 1 cup)
- 1 can Pillsbury Grands! Homestyle refrigerated buttermilk biscuits (5 biscuits)
- 1 tablespoon butter, melted
- ⅓ cup chopped peanuts

1 In large resealable food-storage plastic bag, shake flour and garlic-pepper blend. Add pork; seal bag and shake to coat.

2 In 5-quart ovenproof Dutch oven or saucepot, heat oil over medium heat. Cook pork in oil, stirring occasionally, until golden brown. Stir in squash, peanut sauce, broth and pepper flakes. Heat to boiling; reduce heat to low. Cover; simmer 20 to 25 minutes, stirring occasionally and scraping browned bits from bottom of pan, until pork and squash are tender.

3 Heat oven to 375°F. Add bell pepper and peas to pork mixture; heat to boiling. Separate dough into 5 biscuits; cut each biscuit in half. Dip rounded side of each biscuit half into melted butter and then peanuts. Arrange biscuit halves, cut side down, around outer edges of stew.

4 Bake 20 to 25 minutes or until biscuits are golden brown (do not underbake).

1 Serving: Calories 760; Total Fat 39g (Saturated Fat 11g, Trans Fat 0g); Cholesterol 90mg; Sodium 1980mg; Total Carbohydrate 61g (Dietary Fiber 5g); Protein 41g **Exchanges:** 4 Starch, ½ Vegetable, 4 Lean Meat, 5 Fat **Carbohydrate Choices:** 4

spicy pork chimichurri-style casserole

prep time: 30 Minutes • **start to finish:** 1 Hour 30 Minutes • 5 servings

- 2 tablespoons olive oil
- 2 tablespoons all-purpose flour
- 1 teaspoon salt
- ½ teaspoon paprika
- ¼ teaspoon black pepper
- 1 pork tenderloin (about 1 lb), cut into ¾-inch cubes
- 1 large onion, halved, cut into ½-inch-thick wedges
- 1 lb unpeeled small red potatoes, quartered (2½ cups)
- ¾ to 1 lb sweet potatoes (about 2 medium), peeled, cut into 1½-inch pieces (3 cups)
- 1 cup chopped fresh parsley
- 2 tablespoons chopped fresh oregano leaves
- 2 tablespoons fresh lime juice
- ½ teaspoon crushed red pepper flakes
- 2 cloves garlic, finely chopped
- 1¾ cups chicken broth (from 32-oz carton)
- 1 can Pillsbury Grands! Jr. Golden Layers refrigerated biscuits (10 biscuits)
- ¼ cup finely chopped fresh cilantro

1 Heat oven to 350°F. In 3- or 4-quart ovenproof Dutch oven saucepot, heat oil over medium-high heat. In large shallow bowl, mix flour, salt, paprika and black pepper. Stir in pork until evenly coated. Add to hot oil; cook and stir until evenly browned. Add remaining ingredients except biscuits and cilantro, including any unused flour mixture; mix well.

2 If handles of Dutch oven are not ovenproof, wrap them in foil. Cover Dutch oven; bake 40 minutes. Remove Dutch oven from oven; increase oven temperature to 375°F.

3 Separate dough into 10 biscuits; arrange on top of hot pork mixture. Bake uncovered 14 to 18 minutes longer or until biscuits are golden brown. Sprinkle with cilantro.

1 Serving: Calories 550; Total Fat 19g (Saturated Fat 4g; Trans Fat 3g); Cholesterol 40mg; Sodium 1630mg; Total Carbohydrate 66g (Dietary Fiber 5g); Protein 28g **Exchanges:** 3 Starch, 1½ Other Carbohydrate, 2½ Lean Meat, 2 Fat **Carbohydrate Choices:** 4½

Easy Success Tips

One pound of boneless pork shoulder can be substituted for the pork tenderloin.

Chimichurri originated in Argentina as a sauce or marinade for grilled meats. It is typically served as an accompaniment, but we've used the ingredients to flavor this casserole.

biscuit pepperoni pizza bake

prep time: 10 Minutes • **start to finish:** 40 Minutes • 6 servings

- 1 can Pillsbury Grands! Flaky Layers Original refrigerated biscuits (8 biscuits)
- 1 can (8 oz) pizza sauce
- 2 cups finely shredded mozzarella cheese (8 oz)
- 16 slices pepperoni

1 Heat oven to 375°F. Spray 13x9-inch (3-quart) baking dish with cooking spray. Separate dough into 8 biscuits. Cut each biscuit into 8 pieces; place in medium bowl. Add pizza sauce and 1 cup of the cheese; toss to coat.

2 Spoon and spread mixture in dish. Top with pepperoni and remaining 1 cup cheese.

3 Bake 20 to 23 minutes or until filling is bubbly and biscuits are golden brown.

1 Serving: Calories 430; Total Fat 22g (Saturated Fat 10g, Trans Fat 0g); Cholesterol 35mg; Sodium 1190mg; Total Carbohydrate 38g (Dietary Fiber 0g); Protein 18g **Exchanges:** 1 Starch, 1½ Other Carbohydrate, 2 Medium-Fat Meat, 2½ Fat **Carbohydrate Choices:** 2½

ham and broccoli au gratin

prep time: 10 Minutes • **start to finish:** 35 Minutes • 6 servings

- 2 boxes (10 oz each) frozen broccoli and cheese sauce
- 2 cups diced cooked ham
- ½ cup finely chopped onion
- ¾ cup shredded Italian cheese blend (3 oz)
- 1 can Pillsbury refrigerated crescent dinner rolls (8 rolls) or 1 can Pillsbury refrigerated Crescent Dough Sheet

1 Heat oven to 375°F. Microwave broccoli as directed on box.

2 In medium bowl, mix broccoli and cheese sauce with ham, onion and ½ cup of the cheese. Spoon into ungreased 9-inch round (2-quart) glass baking dish.

3 Remove dough from can but do not unroll. With serrated knife, cut dough into 1-inch slices. Place slices, cut side down, on ham mixture. Sprinkle with remaining ¼ cup cheese.

4 Bake 20 to 25 minutes or until filling is bubbly and dough is golden brown.

1 Serving: Calories 320; Total Fat 18g (Saturated Fat 7g; Trans Fat 2g); Cholesterol 40mg; Sodium 1540mg; Total Carbohydrate 22g (Dietary Fiber 2g); Protein 18g **Exchanges:** 1½ Starch, 2 Lean Meat, 2 Fat **Carbohydrate Choices:** 1½

cheesy sausage breakfast bubble-up bake

prep time: 20 Minutes • **start to finish:** 55 Minutes • 8 servings

- 1 package (12 oz) bulk pork sausage
- ⅓ cup chopped onion
- ⅓ cup chopped green bell pepper
- ⅓ cup chopped red bell pepper
- 10 eggs
- 1 cup shredded Cheddar cheese (4 oz)
- 1 can Pillsbury Grands! Flaky Layers Original refrigerated biscuits (8 biscuits)

1 Heat oven to 375°F. Spray 13x9-inch (3-quart) glass baking dish with cooking spray.

2 In 10-inch skillet, cook sausage, onion and bell peppers over medium-high heat 5 to 7 minutes, stirring occasionally, until pork is no longer pink; drain well.

3 In large bowl, beat eggs. Stir in sausage mixture and cheese. Separate dough into 8 biscuits; press biscuits in bottom of baking dish. Spoon sausage mixture over biscuit crust.

4 Bake 25 to 30 minutes or until egg mixture is set and crust is deep golden brown. Cool 5 minutes before serving.

1 Serving: Calories 410; Total Fat 26g (Saturated Fat 9g; Trans Fat 3.5g); Cholesterol 295mg; Sodium 870mg; Total Carbohydrate 25g (Dietary Fiber 0g); Protein 19g **Exchanges:** 1 Starch, ½ Other Carbohydrate, 2½ Medium-Fat Meat, 2½ Fat **Carbohydrate Choices:** 1½

chili–cheese dog crescent casserole

prep time: 10 Minutes • **start to finish:** 30 Minutes • 6 servings

- 2 cans (15 oz each) chili with beans
- 8 hot dogs, sliced
- 1½ cups shredded American cheese (6 oz)
- 1 can Pillsbury refrigerated crescent dinner rolls (8 rolls) or 1 can Pillsbury refrigerated Crescent Dough Sheet
- 1 tablespoon sesame seed

1 Heat oven to 375°F. In 2-quart saucepan, mix chili and hot dogs. Heat to boiling over medium-high heat, stirring occasionally. Spoon mixture into ungreased 13x9-inch (3-quart) glass baking dish; sprinkle with cheese.

2 If using crescent rolls: Unroll dough; separate into 4 rectangles. Firmly press perforations to seal. If using dough sheet; unroll dough; cut into 4 rectangles. Place rectangles on top of chili mixture. Sprinkle with sesame seed.

3 Bake 15 to 20 minutes or until filling is bubbly and crust is golden brown.

1 Serving: Calories 550; Total Fat 34g (Saturated Fat 15g; Trans Fat 0.5g); Cholesterol 60mg; Sodium 1630mg; Total Carbohydrate 40g (Dietary Fiber 5g); Protein 21g **Exchanges:** 2 Starch, ½ Other Carbohydrate, 2 Medium-Fat Meat, 4½ Fat **Carbohydrate Choices:** 2½

chicken-asiago-spinach quiche

prep time: 30 Minutes • **start to finish:** 1 Hour 25 Minutes • 8 servings

- 1 Pillsbury refrigerated pie crust, softened as directed on box
- 2 tablespoons vegetable oil
- ½ teaspoon finely chopped garlic
- 1 medium onion, chopped (½ cup)
- ½ cup cooked real bacon pieces (from a jar or package)
- 1 cup chopped cooked chicken
- 1 box (9 oz) frozen chopped spinach, thawed, squeezed to drain
- 1 container (8 oz) sour cream
- ¼ teaspoon salt
- ¼ teaspoon garlic powder
- ⅛ teaspoon pepper
- 2 cups shredded sharp Cheddar cheese (8 oz)
- 1½ cups shredded Asiago cheese (6 oz)
- 3 eggs
- ½ cup whipping cream

1 Heat oven to 375°F. Unroll pie crust; press firmly against bottom and side of 9-inch or 9½-inch glass deep-dish pie plate; flute edge as desired. Prick bottom of crust several times with fork to prevent excessive browning. Bake 10 minutes; cool.

2 Meanwhile, in 10-inch skillet, heat oil over medium heat. Cook garlic and onion in oil 2 to 3 minutes, stirring occasionally, until onion is tender. Reduce heat. Stir in bacon, chicken and spinach; toss to combine. Transfer mixture to large bowl. Stir in sour cream, salt, garlic powder and pepper until well blended. Stir in cheeses.

3 In small bowl, beat eggs and whipping cream with fork or whisk until well blended. Gently fold egg mixture into spinach mixture until blended. Pour filling into crust-lined pie plate.

4 Bake 15 minutes. Cover crust edge with pie crust shield ring or 2- to 3-inch strip of foil. Bake 20 to 25 minutes longer or until center is set and crust is golden brown. Let stand 15 minutes before cutting.

1 Serving: Calories 550; Total Fat 43g (Saturated Fat 22g, Trans Fat 1g); Cholesterol 180mg; Sodium 860mg; Total Carbohydrate 17g (Dietary Fiber 0g); Protein 23g **Exchanges:** 1 Starch, 1 Lean Meat, 2 Medium-Fat Meat, 6 Fat **Carbohydrate Choices:** 1

simple spanakopita pie

prep time: 30 Minutes • **start to finish:** 1 Hour 20 Minutes • 6 servings

- 2 boxes (9 oz each) frozen chopped spinach
- 1 container Pillsbury Gluten Free refrigerated pie and pastry dough
- 3 eggs
- 1 cup crumbled feta cheese (4 oz)
- ½ cup whole milk ricotta cheese
- ½ cup sliced green onions (8 medium)
- 2 tablespoons garlic and dill snack and dip seasoning mix (from 3.7-oz jar)

1 Heat oven to 425°F. Microwave frozen spinach as directed on box 6 to 8 minutes to thaw. Drain well; squeeze dry with paper towels.

2 Knead dough until softened and no longer crumbly. Divide dough in half; flatten into 2 rounds. Place 1 round between 2 sheets of cooking parchment or waxed paper. Roll into a round 1½ inches larger than top of 9-inch glass pie plate. Carefully peel off top sheet of paper. Replace paper to cover loosely; carefully turn dough over, and remove second sheet of paper. Use paper to carefully turn dough over into ungreased pie plate; remove paper. Press dough firmly against bottom and up side of pie plate. Roll out second crust.

3 In large bowl, beat eggs with fork. Transfer 1 teaspoon beaten egg to small bowl; set aside. Add spinach, feta cheese, ricotta cheese, onions and seasoning mix to eggs in large bowl; mix until blended. Spread into crust-lined pie plate. Top with second crust; trim edges and lightly crimp with fork.

4 Brush reserved egg on top crust. Cut 4 small slits in top. Cover crust edge with pie crust shield ring or 2- to 3-inch strip of foil to prevent excess browning.

5 Bake 30 to 35 minutes or until golden brown. Cool 15 minutes before cutting.

1 Serving: Calories 820; Total Fat 55g (Saturated Fat 21g; Trans Fat 0g); Cholesterol 120mg; Sodium 1360mg; Total Carbohydrate 69g (Dietary Fiber 3g); Protein 12g
Exchanges: 1 Starch, 3½ Other Carbohydrate, ½ Vegetable, 1 Medium-Fat Meat, 10 Fat
Carbohydrate Choices: 4½

Easy Success Tips

If you can't find the garlic and dill snack and dip seasoning mix, use 1 tablespoon ranch dressing and seasoning mix.

If you are cooking gluten free, always read labels to make sure each recipe ingredient is gluten free. Products and ingredient sources can change.

leek quiche

prep time: 25 Minutes • **start to finish:** 1 Hour 15 Minutes • 6 servings

- 1 Pillsbury refrigerated pie crust, softened as directed on box
- 2 tablespoons butter
- 2 medium leeks, cut in half lengthwise, then cut into ½-inch slices (about 4 cups)
- 3 eggs
- 1 cup milk
- 1 cup shredded Swiss cheese (4 oz)
- ½ teaspoon salt
- ¼ teaspoon pepper
- ⅛ teaspoon ground nutmeg
- Fresh oregano sprig, if desired

1 Heat oven to 400°F. Place pie crust in 9-inch glass pie plate as directed on box for One-Crust Filled Pie. Bake about 8 minutes or until very lightly browned.

2 Meanwhile, in 12-inch skillet, melt butter over medium heat. Cook leeks in butter 7 to 9 minutes, stirring frequently, until tender but not browned. Remove from heat; set aside.

3 In medium bowl, beat eggs with whisk. Stir in milk, cheese, salt, pepper and nutmeg until blended. Stir in leeks. Pour mixture into partially baked crust.

4 Bake 10 minutes. Cover crust edge with pie crust shield ring or 2- to 3-inch strip of foil to prevent excessive browning. Reduce oven temperature to 300°F; bake 20 to 25 minutes longer or until knife inserted in center comes out clean. Let stand 15 minutes before cutting. Garnish with oregano.

1 Serving: Calories 320; Total Fat 20g (Saturated Fat 10g; Trans Fat 0g); Cholesterol 140mg; Sodium 490mg; Total Carbohydrate 23g (Dietary Fiber 0g); Protein 11g
Exchanges: 1½ Starch, ½ Vegetable, ½ Medium-Fat Meat, ½ High-Fat Meat, 2½ Fat
Carbohydrate Choices: 1½

Easy Success Tip

Leeks look like giant green onions and are related to both onions and garlic. Choose leeks that are firm and bright colored with an unblemished white bulb portion. Smaller leeks will be more tender than larger ones. Be sure to wash leeks thoroughly because there is often sand between the layers.

ham and cheddar crouton frittata

prep time: 30 Minutes • **start to finish:** 1 Hour 10 Minutes • 6 servings

- 1 can Pillsbury refrigerated crusty French loaf
- 2 tablespoons butter
- ¼ teaspoon Italian seasoning
- 10 eggs
- ¼ cup milk
- ¼ teaspoon salt
- ⅛ teaspoon pepper
- 1½ cups diced cooked ham
- ½ cup chopped drained roasted red bell peppers (from a jar)
- ½ cup shredded Cheddar cheese (2 oz)
- 2 tablespoons sliced green onions (2 medium)

1 Heat oven to 350°F. Bake loaf as directed on can. Cool completely. With serrated knife, cut half of loaf into ½-inch cubes (about 4 cups). Save remaining half for another use.

2 In 12-inch nonstick ovenproof skillet, melt 1 tablespoon of the butter over medium-high heat. Cook bread cubes and Italian seasoning in butter 3 to 5 minutes, stirring frequently, until golden brown. Remove from skillet to plate; set aside.

3 Increase oven temperature to 400°F. In large bowl, beat eggs, milk, salt and pepper with whisk until well mixed. Stir in ham and roasted peppers. In same skillet, melt remaining 1 tablespoon butter over medium-low heat. Add egg mixture; cook 5 to 7 minutes or until only a thin layer of uncooked eggs remains on top. Remove from heat. Sprinkle bread cubes over egg mixture, pressing lightly with back of spoon.

4 Bake 10 to 15 minutes or until knife inserted in center comes out clean. Sprinkle with cheese. Bake 2 to 3 minutes longer or until cheese is melted. Sprinkle with onions. Cool 10 minutes before cutting.

1 Serving: Calories 390; Total Fat 21g (Saturated Fat 8g, Trans Fat 0g); Cholesterol 350mg; Sodium 1030mg; Total Carbohydrate 27g (Dietary Fiber 0g); Protein 25g **Exchanges:** 1½ Starch, ½ Other Carbohydrate, 1 Very Lean Meat, 1 Lean Meat, ½ High-Fat Meat, 2½ Fat **Carbohydrate Choices**: 2

chicken souvlaki pot pie

prep time: 25 Minutes • **start to finish:** 1 Hour • 6 servings

- 2 tablespoons olive or vegetable oil
- 1¼ lbs boneless skinless chicken breasts, cut into bite-size strips
- 1 medium red onion, chopped (about 1¼ cups)
- 2 small zucchini, cut in half lengthwise, then cut crosswise into slices (about 2⅓ cups)
- 2 cloves garlic, finely chopped
- 2 teaspoons chili powder
- 1½ teaspoons dried oregano leaves
- ½ teaspoon salt
- 1 can (14.5 oz) diced tomatoes, undrained
- ½ cup plain yogurt
- 2 tablespoons all-purpose flour
- 1 Pillsbury refrigerated pie crust, softened as directed on box

Easy Success Tip

Stirring flour into the yogurt before the mixture is added to the chicken filling allows the sauce to thicken when heated without separating.

1 Heat oven to 400°F. In 12-inch nonstick skillet, heat 1 tablespoon of the oil over medium-high heat. Add chicken; cook about 8 minutes, stirring occasionally, until no longer pink in center. Remove chicken from skillet.

2 Heat remaining 1 tablespoon oil in skillet. Add onion and zucchini; cook and stir about 6 minutes or until zucchini is crisp-tender. Return chicken to skillet (discard chicken juices). Stir in garlic, chili powder, oregano and salt. Cook and stir 2 minutes. Stir in tomatoes; cook until thoroughly heated. Remove from heat.

3 In small bowl, beat yogurt and flour with whisk until blended; stir into chicken mixture. Spoon into ungreased 9-inch glass pie plate.

4 Unroll pie crust over hot chicken mixture. Fold excess crust under and press to form thick crust edge; flute. Cut slits in several places in crust. Place pie plate on cookie sheet with sides.

5 Bake 25 to 30 minutes or until crust is golden brown (sauce may bubble slightly over crust). Let stand 5 minutes before serving.

1 Serving: Calories 360; Total Fat 17g (Saturated Fat 5g; Trans Fat 0g); Cholesterol 65mg; Sodium 510mg; Total Carbohydrate 26g (Dietary Fiber 2g); Protein 23g **Exchanges:** 1 Starch, ½ Other Carbohydrate, 1 Vegetable, 2½ Lean Meat, 2 Fat **Carbohydrate Choices:** 2

mexican chicken pot pies in crescent bowls

prep time: 30 Minutes • **start to finish:** 30 Minutes • 4 servings

- 1 can Pillsbury refrigerated Crescent Dough Sheet
- 2 tablespoons butter
- ¼ cup chopped onion
- 1 tablespoon all-purpose flour
- ¼ teaspoon salt
- ⅛ teaspoon pepper
- 1 cup chicken broth
- 1 package (6 oz) refrigerated cooked Southwest-flavor chicken breast strips, coarsely chopped
- 1 can (15 oz) black beans, drained, rinsed
- 3 tablespoons chopped green chiles (from 4.5-oz can), drained
- 1 cup frozen whole kernel corn (from 12-oz bag)
- ½ cup shredded Cheddar-Jack with jalapeño peppers cheese blend (2 oz)
- ½ cup chunky-style salsa

1 Heat oven to 375°F. Place 4 (6-oz) custard cups upside down on cookie sheet with sides. Spray cups with cooking spray.

2 Unroll dough on work surface; starting at center, press dough into 12x8-inch rectangle. Cut into 4 squares. Place 1 dough square over each custard cup, stretching to fit bowl.

3 Bake 12 to 15 minutes or until golden brown. Cool 5 minutes. Remove crescent bowls from custard cups to cooling rack.

4 Meanwhile, in 2-quart saucepan, melt butter over medium heat. Cook onion in butter about 2 minutes, stirring occasionally, until tender. Add flour, salt and pepper; stir until well blended. Gradually stir in broth; cook and stir until bubbly and thickened. Stir in chicken, beans, chiles and corn. Simmer about 5 minutes or until hot.

5 Spoon about ¾ cup chicken mixture into each crescent bowl. Top evenly with cheese and salsa.

1 Serving: Calories 550; Total Fat 22g (Saturated Fat 11g; Trans Fat 0g); Cholesterol 50mg; Sodium 1440mg; Total Carbohydrate 63g (Dietary Fiber 11g); Protein 25g **Exchanges:** 2½ Starch, 1½ Other Carbohydrate, 2½ Lean Meat, 2½ Fat **Carbohydrate Choices:** 4

Easy Success Tip

For more heat in this dish, substitute chopped chipotle chiles in adobo sauce (from 7-ounce can) for the green chiles.

mini chicken alfredo pot pies

prep time: 30 Minutes • **start to finish:** 50 Minutes • 8 pot pies

- 4 cups chopped cooked chicken
- 4 cups frozen mixed vegetables (from two 12-oz bags), thawed, well drained
- 1 jar (16 oz) Alfredo pasta sauce
- ½ cup milk
- ¼ cup grated Parmesan cheese
- 1 box Pillsbury refrigerated pie crusts, softened as directed on box
- 1 egg, beaten

1 Heat oven to 400°F. Place 8 (10-oz) individual baking dishes (ramekins) or custard cups on large cookie sheet with sides.

2 In 3-quart saucepan, place chicken, vegetables, Alfredo sauce, milk and cheese; cook over medium heat, stirring occasionally, until thoroughly heated. Spoon mixture into baking dishes.

3 Unroll pie crusts on lightly floured surface. Cut 4 (4-inch) rounds from each crust. Place 1 dough round over filling on each baking dish; seal edges with fork. Cut slits in crusts. Brush with egg.

4 Bake 15 minutes. Cover loosely with foil; bake about 5 minutes longer or until crust is golden brown.

1 Pot Pie: Calories 490; Total Fat 26g (Saturated Fat 10g; Trans Fat 0g); Cholesterol 0mg; Sodium 690mg; Total Carbohydrate 35g (Dietary Fiber 1g); Protein 28g **Exchanges:** 1½ Starch, 2 Vegetable, 3 Very Lean Meat, 4½ Fat **Carbohydrate Choices:** 1½

Easy Success Tip

These pot pies can be made ahead. Prepare the recipe as directed through step 3—except do not brush with egg. Wrap pot pies individually in plastic wrap and heavy-duty foil; freeze up to 2 months. Thaw in refrigerator overnight. Unwrap, brush with egg and bake as directed.

turkey-vegetable pot pie

prep time: 25 Minutes • **start to finish:** 45 Minutes • 6 servings

- 1 tablespoon butter
- 1 tablespoon olive oil
- ¾ cup sliced carrot
- ¾ cup cubed peeled sweet potato
- ¾ cup sliced peeled parsnip
- ½ cup chopped red onion
- 2 cans (10¾ oz each) condensed cream of chicken soup
- 1½ cups milk
- 1 teaspoon chopped fresh thyme leaves
- ¼ teaspoon salt
- ¼ teaspoon freshly ground pepper
- 3 cups chopped cooked turkey
- 1 can Pillsbury refrigerated Crescent Dough Sheet
- 1 tablespoon butter, melted

1 Heat oven to 375°F. Spray 11x7-inch (2-quart) glass baking dish with cooking spray.

2 In 12-inch skillet, heat 1 tablespoon butter and the oil over medium-high heat. Add carrot, sweet potato, parsnip and onion; cook 10 minutes, stirring occasionally, until vegetables are lightly browned and crisp-tender.

3 In large bowl, stir together soup, milk, thyme, salt and pepper. Stir in turkey and cooked vegetables. Pour into baking dish.

4 Unroll dough on cutting board; cut into strips with fluted pastry wheel or pizza cutter. Arrange strips in lattice design over turkey mixture. Brush dough with melted butter.

5 Bake 15 to 20 minutes or until filling is bubbly and crust is golden brown.

1 Serving: Calories 450; Total Fat 20g (Saturated Fat 8g; Trans Fat 0g); Cholesterol 0mg; Sodium 1230mg; Total Carbohydrate 36g (Dietary Fiber 4g); Protein 29g **Exchanges:** 1½ Starch, ½ Other Carbohydrate, ½ Vegetable, 3 Very Lean Meat, 4 Fat **Carbohydrate Choices:** 2

mini turkey-cranberry pot pies

prep time: 35 Minutes • **start to finish:** 1 Hour 30 Minutes • 6 pot pies

- 2 cups cubed peeled butternut squash (about 9 oz)
- 3 cups cubed cooked turkey
- ¾ cup turkey gravy (from 12-oz jar)
- 3 cups loosely packed fresh baby spinach leaves
- 1 cup cooked wild rice (from 15-oz can)
- ½ cup dried cranberries
- ¼ teaspoon dried thyme leaves
- 1 Pillsbury refrigerated pie crust, softened as directed on box

Easy Success Tip

To shorten prep time, look for ready-to-use squash cubes in the produce aisle or freezer case of your grocery store.

1 Heat oven to 400°F. Line 15x10x1-inch pan with foil. Place 6 (6-oz) individual baking dishes (ramekins) or custard cups in pan.

2 In 1½-quart saucepan, heat squash and ¼ cup water to boiling; reduce heat. Cover; simmer about 6 minutes or until squash is almost tender when pierced with fork. Drain.

3 In large bowl, gently stir squash, turkey, gravy, spinach, wild rice, cranberries, and thyme until well mixed. Divide mixture among baking dishes (dishes will be very full).

4 Unroll pie crust on work surface. Using 4½-inch round cutter, cut 4 rounds from crust; reroll crust and cut 2 more rounds. With paring knife, cut 1½-inch cross shape in center of each round. Place 1 round on top of each dish, stretching if necessary to cover filling. Fold edge of crust under; press lightly onto edge of dish. Gently fold back points of dough from center, forming opening.

5 Bake 15 minutes. Place sheet of foil loosely over pot pies. Bake 25 to 30 minutes longer or until filling is bubbly and crust is golden brown. Cool 10 minutes before serving.

1 Pot Pie: Calories 350; Total Fat 13g (Saturated Fat 4.5g, Trans Fat 0g); Cholesterol 75mg; Sodium 470mg; Total Carbohydrate 36g (Dietary Fiber 2g); Protein 21g **Exchanges:** 2 Starch, ½ Vegetable, 1 Lean Meat, 1 Medium-Fat Meat, 1 Fat **Carbohydrate Choices:** 2½

curried beef and potato mini pies

prep time: 45 Minutes • **start to finish:** 1 Hour 20 Minutes • 12 pies

- ½ lb lean (at least 80%) ground beef
- ¼ cup chopped onion
- 1 cup refrigerated seasoned diced potatoes (from 20-oz bag), coarsely chopped
- ½ cup frozen sweet peas (from 12-oz bag)
- ¾ cup beef gravy (from 12-oz jar)
- 1 teaspoon curry powder
- 1 box Pillsbury refrigerated pie crusts, softened as directed on box
- 2 teaspoons butter, melted
- 1 tablespoon chopped fresh cilantro
- Chutney, if desired

1 Heat oven to 400°F. Spray large cookie sheet with cooking spray.

2 In 10-inch nonstick skillet, cook beef and onion over medium-high heat 5 to 7 minutes, stirring occasionally, until beef is no longer pink; drain. Stir in potatoes, peas, gravy and curry powder. Reduce heat to medium-low. Cover; cook 2 to 3 minutes, stirring occasionally, until potatoes are thoroughly heated. Remove from heat.

3 Unroll pie crusts on work surface. Using 4-inch round cutter, cut 6 rounds from each crust, rerolling dough as necessary. Spread about ¼ cup beef mixture on half of each dough round to within ½ inch of edge. Fold rounds in half; press edges with fork to seal. Cut slits in top of each pie. Place on cookie sheet.

4 Bake 16 to 22 minutes or until golden brown. Immediately brush pies with melted butter; sprinkle with cilantro. Remove from pan to serving plate. Cool 10 minutes. Serve warm with chutney.

1 Pie: Calories 200; Total Fat 11g (Saturated Fat 4.5g, Trans Fat 0g); Cholesterol 15mg; Sodium 290mg; Total Carbohydrate 20g (Dietary Fiber 0g); Protein 5g **Exchanges:** ½ Starch, 1 Other Carbohydrate, ½ Very Lean Meat, 2 Fat **Carbohydrate Choices:** 1

Easy Success Tip

If you like a spicier curry, try hot or Madras curry powder.

ground beef pot pie

prep time: 25 Minutes • **start to finish:** 1 Hour 10 Minutes • 6 servings

- 1 box Pillsbury refrigerated pie crusts, softened as directed on box
- 1 lb lean (at least 80%) ground beef
- 1 medium onion, chopped (½ cup)
- 1 teaspoon garlic salt
- ½ teaspoon pepper
- 3 tablespoons cornstarch
- 3 cups frozen southern-style diced hash brown potatoes (from 32-oz bag), thawed
- 3 medium carrots, sliced (1½ cups)
- 1 jar (12 oz) beef gravy

1 Heat oven to 450°F. Make pie crusts as directed on box for Two-Crust Pie using 9-inch glass pie plate.

2 In 12-inch skillet, cook beef, onion, garlic salt and pepper over medium-high heat 5 to 7 minutes, stirring occasionally, until beef is thoroughly cooked; drain. Stir in cornstarch until mixed. Stir in potatoes, carrots and gravy. Cook 5 to 6 minutes over medium-high heat, stirring constantly, until hot.

3 Spoon beef mixture into crust-lined pie plate. Top with second crust; seal edge and flute. Cut slits in several places in top crust.

4 Bake 15 minutes. Cover crust edge with pie crust shield ring or 2- to 3-inch strip of foil to prevent excessive browning. Bake 20 to 25 minutes longer or until crust is golden brown. Let stand 5 minutes before cutting.

1 Serving: Calories 530; Total Fat 26g (Saturated Fat 11g; Trans Fat 0.5g); Cholesterol 55mg; Sodium 920mg; Total Carbohydrate 55g (Dietary Fiber 3g); Protein 19g **Exchanges:** 3½ Starch, ½ Vegetable, 1 Medium-Fat Meat, 3½ Fat **Carbohydrate Choices:** 3½

Easy Success Tips

Use your own blend of spices instead of garlic salt and pepper, if desired. Seasoned salt, Italian seasoning or grill seasonings work well to flavor meat-and-potato dishes like this.

The filling can be made a day ahead and refrigerated in a tightly covered container. When ready to bake, you may need to add a little extra baking time.

chicken, kale and tomato galette

prep time: 30 Minutes • **start to finish:** 1 Hour • 8 servings

- 1 Pillsbury refrigerated pie crust, softened as directed on box
- ½ cup sun-dried tomato pesto (from 8.5-oz jar)
- 2 tablespoons olive oil
- ½ cup chopped onion
- 1 clove garlic, finely chopped
- 6 cups loosely packed fresh kale-spinach blend
- 2 cups shredded deli rotisserie chicken (from 2-lb chicken)
- ¼ teaspoon pepper
- ½ cup shredded Italian cheese blend (2 oz)
- 1 medium plum (Roma) tomato, thinly sliced
- 1 tablespoon chopped fresh basil leaves
- 1 egg, beaten

1 Heat oven to 375°F. Line large cookie sheet with cooking parchment paper. Unroll pie crust on cookie sheet. Spread 1 tablespoon of the pesto over crust to within 1¼ inches of edge.

2 In 12-inch skillet, heat oil over medium heat. Cook onion and garlic in oil 1 to 2 minutes, stirring frequently, until tender. Stir in kale-spinach blend, chicken, pepper and remaining pesto. Cook 2 to 3 minutes, stirring frequently, until greens are wilted and chicken is thoroughly heated.

3 Spoon chicken mixture over center of crust to within 1¼ inches of edge. Sprinkle with cheese. Fold edge of crust over filling, pleating crust as necessary. Top with tomato, overlapping slices slightly to fit if necessary. Brush crust edge with egg.

4 Bake 20 to 25 minutes or until crust is golden brown. Sprinkle with basil and let stand 5 minutes before cutting.

1 Serving: Calories 340; Total Fat 23g (Saturated Fat 7g, Trans Fat 0g); Cholesterol 65mg; Sodium 500mg; Total Carbohydrate 17g (Dietary Fiber 1g); Protein 16g **Exchanges:** 1 Starch, ½ Vegetable, 1 Very Lean Meat, ½ High-Fat Meat, 3½ Fat **Carbohydrate Choices:** 1

Easy Success Tips

You can use all kale or all spinach instead of a blend of greens.

Any leftover cooked chicken—roasted, grilled or poached—can be substituted for the rotisserie chicken.

Bake-Off® Contest 44, 2010 | **Mary Louise Lever** | Rome, GA

bistro-style onion and artichoke galette

prep time: 25 Minutes • **start to finish:** 1 Hour 5 Minutes • 8 servings

- 1 tablespoon vegetable oil
- 2 cups thinly sliced sweet onion (such as Maui or Walla Walla; about 1 large)
- 2 tablespoons balsamic vinegar
- ½ teaspoon salt-free garlic-and-herb seasoning blend, if desired
- 1 Pillsbury refrigerated pie crust, softened as directed on box
- 1½ teaspoons Dijon mustard
- 4 oz Gruyère cheese, shredded (1 cup)
- 1 jar (6 oz) marinated artichoke hearts, well drained, coarsely chopped
- ¼ cup chopped well-drained fire-roasted red bell peppers (from 7.5-oz jar)
- ⅛ teaspoon crushed red pepper
- 1 teaspoon finely chopped fresh thyme leaves
- 1 egg white, beaten
- Fresh thyme sprigs

1 In 10-inch nonstick skillet, heat oil over medium-high heat. Add onion; cook 8 to 10 minutes, stirring frequently, until soft and golden brown. Reduce heat to medium. Stir in vinegar and seasoning blend; cook 3 to 6 minutes, stirring frequently, until liquid is absorbed. Remove from heat.

2 Meanwhile, heat oven to 375°F. Unroll pie crust on ungreased nonstick cookie sheet. Lightly brush mustard over crust.

3 Sprinkle ⅔ cup of the cheese over center of crust to within 1¼ inches of edge of crust. Spread onion evenly over cheese; top with artichokes and roasted peppers. Sprinkle with red pepper flakes, 1 teaspoon chopped thyme and remaining ⅓ cup cheese. Fold 1¼-inch edge of crust over filling, pleating crust as necessary. Brush egg white over crust edge. Bake 20 to 25 minutes or until crust is golden brown. Cool 15 minutes.

4 To serve, cut into 8 wedges. Garnish with thyme sprigs. Serve warm.

1 Serving: Calories 210; Total Fat 13g (Saturated Fat 6g; Trans Fat 0g); Cholesterol 40mg; Sodium 260mg; Total Carbohydrate 18g (Dietary Fiber 2g); Protein 6g **Exchanges:** 1 Starch, ½ Vegetable, 2½ Fat **Carbohydrate Choices:** 1

CHAPTER 5

bake-shop favorites

french cranberry-apple pie

prep time: 35 Minutes • **start to finish:** 3 Hours 30 Minutes • 8 servings

Crust

1 Pillsbury refrigerated pie crust, softened as directed on box

Filling

4 cups sliced peeled cooking apples (4 medium)

2 cups fresh or frozen cranberries

½ cup granulated sugar

¼ cup all-purpose flour

¼ cup packed brown sugar

½ teaspoon ground cinnamon

¼ teaspoon ground nutmeg

Topping

½ cup all-purpose flour

⅓ cup packed brown sugar

¼ teaspoon ground cinnamon

Dash nutmeg

¼ cup cold butter

⅓ cup chopped pecans

1 Heat oven to 375°F. Place pie crust in 9-inch glass pie plate as directed on box for One-Crust Filled Pie.

2 In large bowl, gently mix apples and cranberries. In small bowl, mix remaining filling ingredients. Add dry ingredients to fruit; toss to coat. Pour filling into crust-lined pie plate.

3 In small bowl, mix all topping ingredients except butter and pecans. Cut in butter, using pastry blender or fork, until crumbly. Stir in pecans. Sprinkle evenly over filling.

4 Bake 45 to 55 minutes or until apples are tender, and crust and topping are golden brown. After 15 to 20 minutes of baking, cover crust edge with pie crust shield ring or 2- to 3-inch strip of foil to prevent excessive browning. Cool 2 hours. Serve with whipped cream or ice cream, if desired.

1 Serving: Calories 380; Total Fat 15g (Saturated Fat 6g; Trans Fat 0g); Cholesterol 15mg; Sodium 135mg; Total Carbohydrate 59g (Dietary Fiber 3g); Protein 3g **Exchanges:** 1 Starch, 1 Fruit, 2 Other Carbohydrate, 3 Fat **Carbohydrate Choices:** 4

gluten-free caramel apple pie

prep time: 15 Minutes • **start to finish:** 3 Hours 5 Minutes • 8 servings

- 1 container Pillsbury Gluten Free refrigerated pie and pastry dough
- 2 cans (21 oz each) gluten-free apple pie filling with more fruit
- ¼ cup gluten-free caramel topping
- 2 tablespoons chopped pecans, toasted*
- 1 pint (2 cups) vanilla ice cream

Easy Success Tip

If you are cooking gluten free, always read labels to make sure each recipe ingredient is gluten free. Products and ingredient sources can change.

1 Heat oven to 425°F. Divide dough in half. Knead 1 half until softened and no longer crumbly. Flatten into a round; place between 2 sheets of cooking parchment or waxed paper. Roll into a round 1½ inches larger than top of 9½-inch deep-dish glass pie plate.

2 Carefully peel off top sheet of paper. Replace paper to cover loosely; carefully turn dough over and remove second sheet of paper. Use paper to carefully turn dough over into ungreased pie plate; remove paper. Press dough firmly against bottom and up side of plate.

3 Spoon pie filling into pastry-lined pie plate. Repeat kneading and rolling of second half of dough; carefully turn dough over on filling. Trim and fold edges together. Flatten edge with fork or crimp. Cover edge with pie crust shield ring or 2- to 3-inch strip of foil to prevent excessive browning.

4 Bake 30 minutes; remove shield ring or foil. Bake 10 to 20 minutes longer or until crust is golden brown. Cool 2 hours.

5 In 1-cup microwavable measuring cup, mix caramel topping and pecans. Microwave on High 30 to 60 seconds or until warm; stir. Top each slice of pie with ¼ cup ice cream; spoon caramel mixture over top.

*To toast pecans, sprinkle in ungreased skillet. Cook over medium heat 5 to 7 minutes, stirring frequently until nuts begin to brown, then stirring constantly until nuts are light brown.

1 Serving: Calories 780; Total Fat 39g (Saturated Fat 14g; Trans Fat 0g); Cholesterol 15mg; Sodium 740mg; Total Carbohydrate 104g (Dietary Fiber 3g); Protein 3g **Exchanges:** 1 Starch, 6 Other Carbohydrate, 7½ Fat **Carbohydrate Choices:** 7

spiced apple and fig hand pies

prep time: 25 Minutes • **start to finish:** 55 Minutes • 8 pies

- 1 tablespoon butter
- 1½ cups (¼-inch pieces) chopped peeled Granny Smith apples
- ¼ cup honey or agave nectar
- ½ teaspoon apple pie spice
- ½ cup (¼-inch pieces) chopped dried figs
- ¼ cup chopped slivered almonds, toasted* if desired
- 1 box Pillsbury refrigerated pie crusts, softened as directed on box
- 1 teaspoon powdered sugar

1 Heat oven to 425°F. In 10-inch nonstick skillet, melt butter over medium heat. Add apples, honey and apple pie spice. Cook 5 to 6 minutes, stirring occasionally, until apples are tender. Remove from heat. Stir in figs and almonds; set aside.

2 Unroll pie crusts on work surface. With 3-inch round cutter, cut 8 rounds from one crust. With 3¼-inch cutter, cut 8 rounds from second crust. Place 3-inch rounds 2 inches apart on large ungreased cookie sheet. Spoon about 3 tablespoons filling onto each round to within ¼ inch of edge; top with 3¼-inch rounds. Press edges firmly with fork to seal. Cut slits in top crusts.

3 Bake 12 to 16 minutes or until golden brown. Cool 10 minutes. Sprinkle with powdered sugar.

*To toast almonds, sprinkle in ungreased skillet. Cook over medium heat 5 to 7 minutes, stirring frequently until almonds begin to brown, then stirring constantly until light brown. Remove from skillet to plate to cool.

1 Pie: Calories 250; Total Fat 11g (Saturated Fat 4.5g, Trans Fat 0g); Cholesterol 10mg; Sodium 210mg; Total Carbohydrate 37g (Dietary Fiber 1g); Protein 1g **Exchanges:** ½ Starch, 2 Other Carbohydrate, 2 Fat **Carbohydrate Choices:** 2½

Easy Success Tips

Pumpkin pie spice can be substituted for the apple pie spice, and dried cherries for the figs.

To sprinkle the powdered sugar evenly over the pies, place it in a small fine-mesh strainer and hold over each pie, gently tapping the edge of the strainer.

three-berry pie

prep time: 25 Minutes • **start to finish:** 3 Hours 25 Minutes • 10 servings

- 1 box Pillsbury refrigerated pie crusts, softened as directed on box
- 1½ cups sugar
- 5 tablespoons cornstarch
- 2 tablespoons quick-cooking tapioca
- ¼ teaspoon salt
- 3 cups fresh blackberries
- 2 cups fresh raspberries
- 2 cups fresh blueberries
- 1 tablespoon milk
- 2 teaspoons sugar

Easy Success Tip

You can use frozen berries in place of fresh, if you like. Partially thaw them before using to help keep their shape during baking. If they are thawed completely, the berries will fall apart when baked.

1 Heat oven to 450°F. Make pie crusts as directed on box for Two-Crust Pie using 9-inch glass pie plate.

2 In large bowl, stir together 1½ cups sugar, the cornstarch, tapioca and salt; add berries and gently toss. Let stand 15 minutes. Spoon into crust-lined pie plate.

3 Cut second crust into ½-inch-wide strips. Arrange strips in lattice design over filling. Trim and seal edges. Brush crust with milk; sprinkle with 2 teaspoons sugar.

4 Place pie on middle oven rack; place large cookie sheet on lower oven rack. Bake 15 minutes. Reduce oven temperature to 375°F. Cover crust edge with pie crust shield ring or 2- to 3-inch strip of foil to prevent excessive browning. Bake 40 to 45 minutes longer or until filling is bubbly and crust is golden brown. Cool 2 hours before serving.

1 Serving: Calories 366; Total Fat 12g (Saturated Fat 5g; Trans Fat 0g); Cholesterol 0mg; Sodium 282mg; Total Carbohydrate 67g (Dietary Fiber 5g); Protein 3g **Exchanges:** 1 Starch, 1 Fruit, 2½ Other Carbohydrate, 2 Fat **Carbohydrate Choices:** 4½

sweet potato pie

prep time: 20 Minutes • **start to finish:** 2 Hours • 8 servings

Crust

1 Pillsbury refrigerated pie crust, softened as directed on box

Filling

1½ cups mashed canned sweet potatoes

⅔ cup packed brown sugar

1 teaspoon ground cinnamon

½ teaspoon ground allspice

1 cup half-and-half

1 tablespoon dry sherry or lemon juice

2 eggs, beaten

Topping

Sweetened whipped cream or whipped topping

1 Heat oven to 425°F. Place pie crust in 9-inch glass pie plate as directed on box for One-Crust Filled Pie.

2 In medium bowl, mix filling ingredients until smooth. Pour into crust-lined pie plate.

3 Bake 15 minutes. Reduce oven temperature to 350°F; bake 30 to 40 minutes longer or until center is set. Cool completely on cooling rack, about 45 minutes. Serve with whipped cream. Store in refrigerator.

1 Serving: Calories 300; Total Fat 12g (Saturated Fat 5g; Trans Fat 0g); Cholesterol 70mg; Sodium 160mg; Total Carbohydrate 45g (Dietary Fiber 1g); Protein 3g **Exchanges:** 1 Starch, 2 Other Carbohydrate, 2½ Fat **Carbohydrate Choices:** 3

Easy Success Tip

For a special touch, pipe the whipped cream onto the pie using a large open star tip. Or save time and use whipped cream topping from an aerosol can.

gluten-free easy pumpkin pie

prep time: 20 Minutes • **start to finish:** 4 Hours 40 Minutes • 8 servings

- ½ container Pillsbury Gluten Free refrigerated pie and pastry dough
- 2 eggs
- 1½ teaspoons pumpkin pie spice
- 1 can (15 oz) pumpkin (not pumpkin pie mix)
- 1 can (14 oz) sweetened condensed milk (not evaporated)
- Sweetened whipped cream, if desired

1 Heat oven to 425°F. Knead dough until softened and no longer crumbly. Flatten into a round; place between 2 sheets of cooking parchment or waxed paper. Roll into a round 1½ inches larger than top of 9-inch glass pie plate.

2 Carefully peel off top sheet of paper. Replace paper to cover loosely; carefully turn dough over, and remove second sheet of paper. Use paper to carefully turn dough over into ungreased pie plate; remove paper. Press dough firmly against bottom and up side of plate. Crimp edge or flatten with fork.

3 In medium bowl, beat eggs slightly with whisk. Beat in pumpkin pie spice, pumpkin and condensed milk. Pour into crust-lined pie plate. Cover edge of crust with pie crust shield ring or 2- to 3-inch strip of foil to prevent excessive browning.

4 Bake 15 minutes. Reduce oven temperature to 350°F; bake about 35 minutes longer or until knife inserted in center comes out clean. Cool on cooling rack 30 minutes. Refrigerate about 3 hours or until chilled. Serve with whipped cream. Store covered in refrigerator.

1 Serving: Calories 430; Total Fat 23g (Saturated Fat 9g; Trans Fat 0g); Cholesterol 65mg; Sodium 420mg; Total Carbohydrate 50g (Dietary Fiber 0g); Protein 6g **Exchanges:** ½ Starch, 2½ Other Carbohydrate, ½ Low-Fat Milk, 4 Fat **Carbohydrate Choices:** 3

Easy Success Tip

If you are cooking gluten free, always read labels to make sure each recipe ingredient is gluten free. Products and ingredient sources can change.

lemon meringue pie

prep time: 30 Minutes • **start to finish:** 5 Hours 15 Minutes • 8 servings

Crust

1 Pillsbury refrigerated pie crust, softened as directed on box

Filling

1¼ cups sugar
⅓ cup cornstarch
½ teaspoon salt
1½ cups cold water
3 egg yolks
2 tablespoons butter
1 tablespoon grated lemon peel
½ cup fresh lemon juice

Meringue

3 egg whites
¼ teaspoon cream of tartar
½ teaspoon vanilla
¼ cup sugar

1 Heat oven to 450°F. Make pie crust as directed on box for One-Crust Baked Shell using 9-inch glass pie plate. Cool completely. Reduce oven temperature to 350°F.

2 Meanwhile, in 2-quart saucepan, mix 1¼ cups sugar, the cornstarch and salt. Gradually stir in cold water until smooth. Cook over medium heat, stirring constantly, until mixture boils. Boil and stir 1 minute. Remove from heat.

3 In small bowl, beat egg yolks. Stir ¼ cup of hot mixture into egg yolks. Gradually stir yolk mixture into hot mixture. Cook over low heat, stirring constantly, until mixture boils. Boil and stir 1 minute. Remove from heat. Stir in butter, lemon peel and lemon juice. Cool 15 minutes. Pour into cooled baked shell.

4 In small deep bowl, beat egg whites, cream of tartar and vanilla with electric mixer on medium speed about 1 minute or until soft peaks form. On high speed, gradually beat in ¼ cup sugar, 1 tablespoon at a time, until stiff glossy peaks form and sugar is dissolved. Spoon meringue onto hot filling; spread to edge of crust to seal well and prevent shrinkage.

5 Bake 12 to 15 minutes or until meringue is light golden brown. Cool completely, 1 hour. Refrigerate until filling is set, about 3 hours. Store in refrigerator.

1 Serving: Calories 340; Total Fat 11g (Saturated Fat 5g, Trans Fat 0g); Cholesterol 80mg; Sodium 330mg; Total Carbohydrate 56g (Dietary Fiber 0g); Protein 3g **Exchanges:** 1 Starch, 2½ Other Carbohydrate, 2 Fat **Carbohydrate Choices:** 4

Easy Success Tip

Egg whites will whip best at room temperature. To take the chill off, set the bowl of whites into a larger pan filled with warm water.

Bake-Off® Contest 12, 1960 | **Mrs. H. G. Alexander, Sr.** | Tampa, FL

chocolate dream pie

prep time: 30 Minutes • **start to finish:** 6 Hours 30 Minutes • 10 servings

- 1 Pillsbury refrigerated pie crust, softened as directed on box
- ½ cup sugar
- ¼ cup cornstarch
- ⅛ teaspoon salt
- 2 egg yolks, slightly beaten
- 1 cup milk
- 1 cup semisweet chocolate chips
- 3 oz (from 8-oz package) cream cheese, cut into cubes, softened
- 1½ cups whipping cream
- 1 teaspoon vanilla

1 Heat oven to 450°F. Make pie crust as directed on box for One-Crust Baked Shell using 9-inch glass pie plate. Cool completely.

2 Meanwhile, in 2-quart saucepan, mix sugar, cornstarch, salt and egg yolks until well blended. Gradually stir in milk. Add chocolate chips. Cook over medium heat, stirring constantly, until chips are melted and mixture thickens and boils. Boil and stir 1 minute. Remove from heat. Beat in cream cheese with whisk until melted and mixture is smooth. Transfer mixture to large bowl; cover surface with plastic wrap. Refrigerate until just cool, about 1 hour.

3 In chilled large, deep bowl, beat whipping cream and vanilla with electric mixer on low speed until mixture begins to thicken. Gradually increase speed to high and beat just until stiff peaks form. (Do not over beat or mixture will curdle.) Reserve 1 cup whipped cream for topping; refrigerate.

4 Fold remaining whipped cream into chocolate filling. Spoon and spread filling into cooled baked shell. Refrigerate 4 to 6 hours or until set (pie will be softly set and will not be firm, but cut slices will retain their shape). Spread or pipe reserved 1 cup whipped cream over filling. Store covered in refrigerator.

1 Serving: Calories 400; Total Fat 26g (Saturated Fat 14g; Trans Fat 0.5g); Cholesterol 95mg; Sodium 170mg; Total Carbohydrate 37g (Dietary Fiber 1g); Protein 3g **Exchanges:** 1 Starch, 1½ Other Carbohydrate, 5 Fat **Carbohydrate Choices:** 2½

dulce de leche–banana pie

prep time: 15 Minutes • **start to finish:** 1 Hour • 8 servings

- 1 Pillsbury refrigerated pie crust, softened as directed on box
- 1 can (13.4 oz) dulce de leche (caramelized sweetened condensed milk)
- 3 ripe medium bananas
- 1 cup whipping cream
- ¼ cup powdered sugar
- ½ cup semisweet chocolate chips
- 1 teaspoon vegetable oil

1 Heat oven to 450°F. Make pie crust as directed on box for One-Crust Baked Shell using 9-inch glass pie plate. Cool completely.

2 Spoon contents of can of dulce de leche into center of cooled baked shell; gently spread to edge. Thinly slice bananas; arrange over dulce de leche.

3 In chilled medium, deep bowl, beat whipping cream and powdered sugar with electric mixer on low speed until mixture begins to thicken. Gradually increase speed to high and beat just until soft peaks form. (Do not over beat or mixture will curdle.) Spread whipped cream over bananas.

4 In small microwavable bowl, microwave chocolate chips and oil uncovered on High 30 to 60 seconds, stirring once, until chips are softened and can be stirred smooth. Drizzle chocolate over whipped cream. Store in refrigerator.

1 Serving: Calories 500; Total Fat 26g (Saturated Fat 12g; Trans Fat 2g); Cholesterol 35mg; Sodium 210mg; Total Carbohydrate 60g (Dietary Fiber 2g); Protein 7g **Exchanges:** 1 Starch, 3 Other Carbohydrate, ½ High-Fat Meat, 4 Fat **Carbohydrate Choices:** 4

creamy cashew turtle pie

prep time: 25 Minutes • **start to finish:** 1 Hour 55 Minutes • 8 servings

- 1 Pillsbury refrigerated pie crust, softened as directed on box
- ¾ cup milk chocolate chips
- 1⅓ cups creamy cashew butter
- 1 cup chopped salted cashews
- 1 package (8 oz) cream cheese, softened
- ⅔ cup caramel topping
- 1 container (8 oz) frozen whipped topping, thawed

Easy Success Tip

Look for cashew butter near the peanut butter or natural products in your grocery store.

1 Heat oven to 450°F. Make pie crust as directed on box for One-Crust Baked Shell using 9-inch glass pie plate. Cool completely.

2 In small microwavable bowl, microwave ½ cup of the chocolate chips uncovered on High 30 to 60 seconds, stirring once, until chips are softened and can be stirred smooth. Add ⅓ cup of the cashew butter; mix well. Spread chocolate mixture over bottom of cooled baked shell. Sprinkle with ¾ cup of the cashews.

3 In large bowl, beat cream cheese, remaining 1 cup cashew butter and the caramel topping with electric mixer on medium speed 1 to 2 minutes or until blended. Gently stir in whipped topping until well blended. Spoon and spread cream cheese mixture over cashews. Refrigerate 1 hour.

4 In small microwavable bowl, microwave remaining ¼ cup chocolate chips uncovered on High 30 to 60 seconds, stirring once, until chips are softened and can be stirred smooth. Drizzle chocolate over pie. Sprinkle with remaining ¼ cup cashews. Refrigerate at least 30 minutes before serving. Store loosely covered in refrigerator.

1 Serving: Calories 830; Total Fat 57g (Saturated Fat 22g; Trans Fat 0g); Cholesterol 40mg; Sodium 590mg; Total Carbohydrate 66g (Dietary Fiber 2g); Protein 13g **Exchanges:** 1 Starch, 3½ Other Carbohydrate, 1½ High-Fat Meat, 9 Fat **Carbohydrate Choices:** 4½

strawberry-rhubarb mini pies

prep time: 30 Minutes • **start to finish:** 1 Hour 10 Minutes • 6 pies

- 2 cups frozen strawberries, thawed, drained and juice reserved
- 1 cup sugar
- 2 tablespoons cornstarch
- 3 cups frozen chopped rhubarb, partially thawed
- 1 box Pillsbury refrigerated pie crusts, softened as directed on box

1 Heat oven to 450°F. In medium bowl, place reserved strawberry juice. In small bowl, mix ⅓ cup of the sugar and the cornstarch. Add to strawberry juice, beating with whisk. Stir in strawberries and rhubarb.

2 Unroll pie crusts on work surface. Cut 3 (3½-inch) rounds and 3 (4¾-inch) rounds from each crust. Firmly press 4¾-inch rounds in bottom and up side of 6 ungreased 6-oz custard cups. Divide fruit mixture evenly among crust-lined cups.

3 Place 3½-inch rounds over filling; crimp edges to seal. Cut slits in tops of pies. Sprinkle evenly with remaining ⅔ cup sugar. Place cups in 15x10x1-inch pan.

4 Bake 32 to 36 minutes or until golden brown. Serve warm.

1 Pie: Calories 670; Total Fat 16g (Saturated Fat 7g; Trans Fat 0g); Cholesterol 10mg; Sodium 350mg; Total Carbohydrate 127g (Dietary Fiber 4g); Protein 3g **Exchanges:** 1 Starch, 1½ Fruit, 6 Other Carbohydrate, 3 Fat **Carbohydrate Choices:** 8½

mini s'mores hand pies

prep time: 35 Minutes • **start to finish:** 50 Minutes • 10 pies

Crust

- **1 box Pillsbury refrigerated pie crusts, softened as directed on box**
- **½ cup graham cracker crumbs**
- **¼ cup sugar**
- **3 tablespoons butter, melted**

Filling

- **½ cup marshmallow creme**
- **2 tablespoons cream cheese spread (from 8-oz container)**
- **2 tablespoons sugar**
- **½ cup semisweet or milk chocolate chips**

1 Heat oven to 425°F. Line cookie sheet with cooking parchment paper.

2 Unroll pie crusts on work surface. With 3-inch round cutter, cut 10 rounds from each crust. In shallow bowl, mix cracker crumbs and ¼ cup sugar. Brush both sides of pie crust rounds with butter; dip into crumb mixture to coat.

3 In small bowl, stir together filling ingredients. Spoon about 1 heaping tablespoon filling onto center of 10 coated rounds. Top with remaining 10 rounds; pinch edges to seal. Place on cookie sheet.

4 Bake 9 to 12 minutes or until golden brown. Serve warm or cool. Store covered in refrigerator.

1 Pie: Calories 320; Total Fat 17g (Saturated Fat 8g; Trans Fat 0g); Cholesterol 20mg; Sodium 280mg; Total Carbohydrate 39g (Dietary Fiber 0g); Protein 2g **Exchanges:** 1½ Starch, 1 Other Carbohydrate, 3 Fat **Carbohydrate Choices:** 2½

black-bottom coconut cream tart

prep time: 40 Minutes • **start to finish:** 4 Hours 20 Minutes • 10 servings

Crust and filling

- 1 Pillsbury refrigerated pie crust, softened as directed on box
- ½ cup dark or semisweet chocolate chips
- 3 tablespoons half-and-half
- 4 egg yolks
- ¾ cup sugar
- ⅓ cup cornstarch
- ½ teaspoon salt
- 1 can (14 oz) coconut milk (not cream of coconut)
- 1 cup half-and-half
- ½ teaspoon coconut extract
- 2 tablespoons butter, softened
- 1½ cups sweetened flaked coconut, toasted*

Topping

- 1½ cups whipping cream
- ¼ cup dark or semisweet chocolate chips
- 1 teaspoon vegetable oil

1 Heat oven to 450°F. Place pie crust in 10-inch tart pan with removable bottom or 9-inch glass pie plate. Bake as directed on box for One-Crust Baked Shell. Cool completely.

2 Meanwhile, in small microwavable bowl, microwave ½ cup chocolate chips and 3 tablespoons half-and-half uncovered on High 20 to 30 seconds, until mixture can be stirred smooth. Refrigerate uncovered 20 minutes. Spread over bottom of cooled baked shell.

3 In medium bowl, beat egg yolks with fork; set aside. In 2-quart saucepan, mix sugar, cornstarch and salt. Gradually stir in coconut milk, 1 cup half-and-half and the coconut extract with whisk. Cook over medium heat 8 to 10 minutes, stirring constantly, until mixture thickens and boils. Boil and stir 1 minute. Immediately stir half of the hot mixture into egg yolks, then stir back into hot mixture in saucepan. Reduce heat to medium-low. Heat to boiling, stirring constantly; boil and stir 1 minute. Remove from heat. Add butter and 1¼ cups of the coconut; stir until butter is melted. Cool 10 minutes. Pour into crust. Press plastic wrap on filling. Refrigerate 3 hours or until set.

4 In chilled large, deep bowl, beat whipping cream with electric mixer on low speed until mixture begins to thicken. Gradually increase speed to high and beat just until soft peaks form. (Do not over beat or mixture will curdle.) Carefully remove plastic wrap from pie. Spread whipped cream over filling; sprinkle with remaining ¼ cup coconut.

5 In small microwavable bowl, microwave ¼ cup chocolate chips and the oil uncovered on High 20 to 40 seconds, stirring once, until chips are softened and mixture can be stirred smooth. Drizzle chocolate over pie.

*To toast coconut, sprinkle in ungreased skillet. Cook over medium-low heat 6 to 14 minutes, stirring frequently until browning begins, then stirring constantly until golden brown.

1 Serving: Calories 590; Total Fat 42g (Saturated Fat 28g, Trans Fat 0.5g); Cholesterol 140mg; Sodium 310mg; Total Carbohydrate 47g (Dietary Fiber 2g); Protein 5g **Exchanges:** 1 Starch, 2 Other Carbohydrate, 8½ Fat **Carbohydrate Choices:** 3

Bake-Off® Contest 47, 2014 | **Brenda Watts** | Gaffney, SC

macaroon–peanut butter–chocolate tartlets

prep time: 30 Minutes • **start to finish:** 1 Hour 10 Minutes • 20 tartlets

- 2 cups flaked coconut
- 1 roll Pillsbury refrigerated peanut butter cookie dough
- 2 containers (8 oz each) mascarpone cheese
- ¾ cup powdered sugar
- 1½ teaspoons coconut extract
- 1 cup whipped peanut butter– and chocolate-flavored spread

1 Heat oven to 350°F. Line cookie sheet with cooking parchment paper. Spread ½ cup of the coconut on cookie sheet. Bake 5 to 7 minutes, stirring occasionally, until golden brown. Remove to plate to cool.

2 Place foil baking cup in each of 20 regular-size muffin cups. In shallow bowl, place remaining 1½ cups coconut. Shape cookie dough into 20 (1½-inch) balls. Roll each ball in coconut, pressing coconut lightly into dough. With floured fingers, press each ball in bottom and halfway up side of muffin cup.

3 Bake 10 to 16 minutes or until golden brown. Cool 3 minutes; remove from pans to cooling racks. Cool completely, about 15 minutes. Remove foil baking cups.

4 In small bowl, beat ½ cup of the mascarpone cheese, ¼ cup of the powdered sugar and ½ teaspoon of the coconut extract with whisk until smooth; set aside.

5 In large bowl, beat remaining 1½ cups mascarpone cheese, the chocolate spread, remaining ½ cup powdered sugar and remaining 1 teaspoon coconut extract with electric mixer on medium speed 1 to 2 minutes or until smooth. Spoon about 2 tablespoons chocolate mixture into each cookie cup. Top with 1 teaspoon mascarpone mixture; sprinkle with toasted coconut. Store covered in refrigerator.

1 Tartlet: Calories 320; Total Fat 22g (Saturated Fat 11g; Trans Fat 0g); Cholesterol 30mg; Sodium 160mg; Total Carbohydrate 27g (Dietary Fiber 0g); Protein 3g **Exchanges:** 2 Other Carbohydrate, ½ Medium-Fat Meat, 4 Fat **Carbohydrate Choices:** 2

gluten-free chocolate tarts

prep time: 25 Minutes • **start to finish:** 1 Hour 25 Minutes • 12 tarts

- ½ container Pillsbury Gluten Free refrigerated pie and pastry dough
- 1 box (4-serving size) gluten-free chocolate pudding and pie filling mix (not instant)
- 1½ cups milk
- 1 cup semisweet chocolate chips
- ¾ cup frozen (thawed) whipped topping or sweetened whipped cream
- Fresh raspberries and chocolate shavings, if desired

1 Heat oven to 425°F. Knead dough until softened and no longer crumbly. Press about 1½ tablespoons dough in bottom and up side of each of 12 ungreased regular-size muffin cups. Prick bottoms several times with fork.

2 Bake 5 minutes. Remove from oven; prick bottoms with fork. Bake 5 to 7 minutes longer or until edges are golden brown. Cool 5 minutes; carefully remove from pan to cooling rack. Cool completely, about 20 minutes.

3 Meanwhile, in 2-quart saucepan, stir pudding mix into milk. Heat to boiling over medium heat, stirring constantly. Reduce heat to low; stir in chocolate chips. Cook and stir until chocolate is melted and mixture is smooth. Remove from heat; cool 15 minutes.

4 Spoon about 2 tablespoons filling into each cooled baked shell. Refrigerate at least 30 minutes to chill. Top each with 1 tablespoon whipped topping. Garnish with raspberries and chocolate.

1 Tart: Calories 300; Total Fat 17g (Saturated Fat 8g; Trans Fat 0g); Cholesterol 0mg; Sodium 280mg; Total Carbohydrate 34g (Dietary Fiber 1g); Protein 2g **Exchanges:** ½ Starch, 2 Other Carbohydrate, 3½ Fat **Carbohydrate Choices:** 2

Easy Success Tips

If you love mint and chocolate, stir ½ teaspoon peppermint extract into the pudding mixture. Unwrap and coarsely chop thin rectangular gluten-free crème de menthe chocolate candies; sprinkle over the whipped topping.

If you are cooking gluten free, always read labels to make sure each recipe ingredient is gluten free. Products and ingredient sources can change.

orange cream–macadamia torte

prep time: 40 Minutes • **start to finish:** 2 Hours 50 Minutes • 16 servings

Torte

- 1 roll Pillsbury refrigerated sugar cookie dough
- 1 package (8 oz) cream cheese, softened
- 1 teaspoon vanilla
- 1¼ cups flaked coconut, toasted*
- 1¼ cups chopped macadamia nuts, toasted*
- 3 tablespoons grated orange peel
- 2 tablespoons grated lemon peel
- 1 can (14 oz) sweetened condensed milk (not evaporated)
- ¼ cup freshly squeezed orange juice
- 2 tablespoons butter

Icing

- 1 cup white vanilla baking chips
- 1 tablespoon shortening

Garnish, if desired

- 1 large orange, cut into 16 thin slices

*To toast coconut, sprinkle in ungreased skillet. Cook over medium-low heat 6 to 14 minutes, stirring frequently until browning begins, then stirring constantly until golden brown.

1 Heat oven to 350°F. Let cookie dough stand at room temperature 10 minutes to soften.

2 In large bowl, break up cookie dough. Add 2 oz of the cream cheese and the vanilla; beat with electric mixer on medium speed until well blended. Add 1 cup of the coconut, ¾ cup of the nuts, 1 tablespoon of the orange peel and 1 tablespoon of the lemon peel; beat until well blended. Spread evenly in bottom and up side of ungreased 10-inch nonstick tart pan with removable bottom.

3 Bake 18 to 23 minutes or until light golden brown. Cool completely on cooling rack, about 1 hour.

4 Meanwhile, in 2-quart saucepan, stir together condensed milk, orange juice, butter, and remaining 6 oz cream cheese, 2 tablespoons orange peel and 1 tablespoon lemon peel. Cook over low heat 20 to 25 minutes, stirring frequently with whisk, until mixture is bubbly and thickened. Remove from heat; spread over cooled crust. Refrigerate until cooled, about 1 hour.

5 In small microwavable bowl, microwave baking chips and shortening uncovered on High 30 to 40 seconds, stirring every 10 seconds, until smooth. Drizzle over torte. Sprinkle with remaining ¼ cup coconut and ½ cup nuts, lightly pressing into icing. Garnish individual servings with orange slices. Store loosely covered in refrigerator.

1 Serving: Calories 450; Total Fat 27g (Saturated Fat 13g; Trans Fat 2g); Cholesterol 30mg; Sodium 250mg; Total Carbohydrate 46g (Dietary Fiber 1g); Protein 5g **Exchanges:** 1½ Starch, 1½ Other Carbohydrate, 5½ Fat **Carbohydrate Choices:** 3

*To toast macadamia nuts, spread in shallow pan. Bake at 350°F for 6 to 10 minutes, stirring occasionally, until light brown.

Baked Doughnut Glazes

Warm doughnuts—everyone loves them. They are super easy to make at home without taking out your rolling pin or deep-fat fryer. With the magic of refrigerated biscuit dough, you can bake doughnuts conveniently in the oven. Just cut a hole out of the middle of each biscuit and bake the doughnuts and doughnut holes as directed in the recipe. Then the only decision remaining is whether to top with a sweet glaze and topping or our colorful icing before taking that big bite. (If you use the glaze or icing, omit the sugar-cinnamon mixture.) Enjoy a batch of these easy doughnuts for breakfast or a snack anytime.

DOUGHNUT GLAZE

Mix desired glaze ingredients in small bowl until smooth. Let doughnuts cool 5 minutes before dipping in glaze.

Top the White and Chocolate Glazes with colored sprinkles, mini chocolate chips or your favorite topping. Top the Maple-Glazed doughnuts with crisply cooked bacon or candied bacon (see Candied Bacon–Peanut Butter Cookies for making candied bacon, page 294).

White Glaze: 1 cup powdered sugar and 4 to 6 teaspoons milk.

Chocolate Glaze: 1 cup powdered sugar, 2 tablespoons unsweetened cocoa powder and 4 to 6 teaspoons milk.

Maple Glaze: 1 cup powdered sugar, 4 to 6 teaspoons milk and ¼ teaspoon maple flavoring.

DOUGHNUT RAINBOW ICING

In large bowl, mix 4½ cups powdered sugar, 6 tablespoons milk and 4 tablespoons light corn syrup until well blended. Icing will be thick. Divide icing evenly into 6 small bowls. Add a different color of gel icing color to each bowl; stir to blend each. Try red, orange, yellow, green, blue and purple or your favorite colors. Let doughnuts cool 5 minutes before topping with icing.

Place each color icing in small resealable food-storage plastic bag. Cut off tiny corner of each bag. Place cooling rack on large cookie sheet; place doughnuts on rack. To make a rainbow on each doughnut, pipe one stripe of red, orange, yellow, green, blue and purple icing over top and slightly over edge of doughnut so that colors just touch. Pipe icing on 1 or 2 doughnuts at a time so icing can blend together slightly before it sets. The icing will spread slightly and drip down sides. Let stand at least 30 minutes or until icing is set.

baked sugar doughnuts

prep time: 10 Minutes • **start to finish:** 30 Minutes • 8 servings

- 1 can Pillsbury Grands! refrigerated biscuits (8 biscuits)
- ¾ cup sugar
- ¾ teaspoon ground cinnamon
- ⅓ cup butter, melted

1 Heat oven to 350°F. Separate dough into 8 biscuits. Place biscuits on work surface. With 1¼-inch round cutter, cut hole in center of each biscuit.

2 In small bowl, mix sugar and cinnamon. Dip all sides of biscuits and centers into butter; shake off excess. Place in bowl of cinnamon-sugar; turn to coat. Place on ungreased large cookie sheet.

3 Bake 14 to 18 minutes or until golden brown. Serve warm.

1 Serving (1 Doughnut and 1 Doughnut Hole): Calories 320; Total Fat 15g (Saturated Fat 6g; Trans Fat 4g); Cholesterol 20mg; Sodium 630mg; Total Carbohydrate 44g (Dietary Fiber 0g); Protein 3g **Exchanges:** 1 Starch, 2 Other Carbohydrate, 3 Fat **Carbohydrate Choices:** 3

Easy Success Tip

To reheat, place 1 doughnut at a time on microwavable plate. Microwave uncovered on Medium (50%) 10 to 20 seconds or just until warm.

citrus-fennel doughnuts

prep time: 40 Minutes • **start to finish:** 40 Minutes • 28 doughnuts

- **1 teaspoon grated orange peel**
- **⅓ cup sugar**
- **½ teaspoon fennel seed, crushed**
- **6 cups vegetable oil**
- **1 can Pillsbury refrigerated Crescent Dough Sheet**

1 Pat excess moisture from orange peel with paper towel. In small spice grinder or small food processor, grind orange peel, sugar and fennel seed until well blended. Transfer to small shallow bowl; set aside.

2 In deep fryer or 3-quart heavy saucepan, heat oil to 350°F. Meanwhile, unroll dough sheet on work surface; starting at center, press dough into 14x8-inch rectangle. Using pizza cutter or knife, cut into 28 (2-inch) squares.

3 Gently place 3 to 4 doughnuts in hot oil. Fry on one side until golden brown. Gently turn with tongs; fry until other side is golden brown. Drain on paper towels.

4 While doughnuts are still warm, add to sugar mixture; turn to coat. Sprinkle doughnuts with remaining sugar mixture.

1 Doughnut: Calories 120; Total Fat 11g (Saturated Fat 2g, Trans Fat 0g); Cholesterol 0mg; Sodium 60mg; Total Carbohydrate 6g (Dietary Fiber 0g); Protein 0g **Exchanges:** ½ Other Carbohydrate, 2 Fat **Carbohydrate Choices:** ½

Easy Success Tip

If you don't have a spice grinder to crush the fennel seed, place it in a small resealable food-storage plastic bag and crush with a meat mallet or rolling pin.

baked banana-cookie doughnuts

prep time: 10 Minutes • **start to finish:** 40 Minutes • 12 doughnuts

- 1 roll Pillsbury refrigerated sugar cookie dough
- 1 medium ripe banana, mashed (½ cup)
- ¼ cup milk
- 1 egg
- 1 teaspoon vanilla
- 2 tablespoons sugar
- 1 teaspoon ground cinnamon

1 Heat oven to 425°F. Spray 2 doughnut pans with cooking spray; lightly sprinkle with flour. Let cookie dough stand at room temperature 10 minutes to soften.

2 In large bowl, break up cookie dough; add banana, milk, egg and vanilla. Beat with electric mixer on medium speed 2 minutes, scraping bowl occasionally. Spoon batter evenly into doughnut cups (cups will be almost full).

3 Bake 7 to 9 minutes or until tops spring back when lightly touched. Cool 10 minutes.

4 In small bowl, mix sugar and cinnamon. Gently run metal spatula around edge of doughnuts to loosen; carefully remove from pans (doughnuts will be very tender). Dip tops of doughnuts in cinnamon-sugar. Serve warm.

1 Doughnut: Calories 190; Total Fat 7g (Saturated Fat 2g, Trans Fat 0g); Cholesterol 20mg; Sodium 135mg; Total Carbohydrate 29g (Dietary Fiber 0g); Protein 2g **Exchanges:** ½ Starch, 1½ Other Carbohydrate, 1½ Fat **Carbohydrate Choices:** 2

Easy Success Tip

For the best flavor and moistness, use heavily speckled, ripe bananas for these doughnuts.

s'mores crescent doughnuts

prep time: 20 Minutes • **start to finish:** 25 Minutes • 3 doughnuts

- 2 cups vegetable oil
- 1 can Pillsbury refrigerated crescent dinner rolls (8 rolls)
- ⅓ cup marshmallow creme (from 7-oz jar)
- ¼ cup milk chocolate chips, melted
- 1½ teaspoons graham cracker crumbs

Easy Success Tip

For easier piping, spray the inside of the bag with cooking spray before adding the marshmallow creme.

1 In deep fryer or 2-quart heavy saucepan, heat oil to 350°F.

2 Meanwhile, separate dough into 4 rectangles; firmly press perforations to seal. Stack 2 rectangles on top of one another. Fold in half widthwise to make tall stack. Repeat with remaining 2 rectangles.

3 To make 2 doughnuts, use 3-inch biscuit cutter to cut 1 round from each stack; use ½-inch biscuit cutter to cut small hole in center of each round. Reroll remaining dough to cut third doughnut.

4 Fry doughnuts in hot oil 3 minutes, gently turning once with tongs, until deep golden brown and cooked through. Drain on paper towels. Cool 5 minutes.

5 Carefully split doughnuts in half. Spoon marshmallow creme into resealable food-storage plastic bag. Cut ½ inch off one corner of bag; pipe marshmallow creme onto doughnut bottoms. Cover with doughnut tops. Spread melted chocolate on tops; sprinkle with graham cracker crumbs.

1 Doughnut: Calories 490; Total Fat 30g (Saturated Fat 10g, Trans Fat 0g); Cholesterol 0mg; Sodium 580mg; Total Carbohydrate 50g (Dietary Fiber 0g); Protein 6g **Exchanges:** 1½ Starch, 2 Other Carbohydrate, 6 Fat **Carbohydrate Choices:** 3

coconut cream–filled doughnut holes

prep time: 25 Minutes • **start to finish:** 55 Minutes • 32 doughnut holes

- 1 can Pillsbury Grands! Homestyle refrigerated buttermilk biscuits (8 biscuits)
- 1 box (4-serving size) coconut cream instant pudding and pie filling mix
- 1¾ cups cold milk
- ¾ cup powdered sugar
- 4 to 5 teaspoons milk
- ⅔ cup flaked coconut, toasted* if desired

Easy Success Tips

Your favorite flavor of pudding can be used instead of the coconut cream.

To make jelly-filled doughnut holes, substitute jelly or fruit spread for the pudding. Omit glaze and coconut; sprinkle tops of doughnuts with powdered sugar.

1 Heat oven to 350°F. Separate dough into 8 biscuits. Cut each biscuit into 4 wedges; roll each wedge into a ball. Place 1 inch apart on large ungreased cookie sheet.

2 Bake 13 to 17 minutes or until light golden brown. Remove from cookie sheet to cooling rack; cool 5 minutes.

3 Meanwhile, in medium bowl, beat pudding mix and cold milk with whisk 2 minutes. With straw, poke hole in side of each doughnut hole almost to other side. Spoon 1 cup of the pudding into decorating bag fitted with ¼-inch round tip. (Refrigerate remaining pudding for another use.) Insert tip in hole of each doughnut; carefully squeeze bag to fill doughnut with pudding.

4 In small bowl, stir powdered sugar and 4 to 5 teaspoons milk until smooth and drizzling consistency. Place coconut in another small bowl. Dip tops of filled doughnut holes in glaze; shake off excess, then dip in coconut. Let stand 5 minutes or until set.

*To toast coconut, sprinkle in ungreased skillet. Cook over medium-low heat 6 to 14 minutes, stirring frequently until browning begins, then stirring constantly until golden brown.

1 Doughnut Hole: Calories 70; Total Fat 2g (Saturated Fat 1g, Trans Fat 0g); Cholesterol 0mg; Sodium 170mg; Total Carbohydrate 13g (Dietary Fiber 0g); Protein 1g **Exchanges:** 1 Other Carbohydrate, ½ Fat **Carbohydrate Choices:** 1

Bake-Off® Contest 46, 2013 | **Karyn Hentz** | Arlington, VA

espresso hazelnut beignets

prep time: 25 Minutes • **start to finish:** 25 Minutes • 8 beignets

- 4 cups vegetable oil
- ¼ cup sugar
- ½ teaspoon instant espresso coffee powder or granules
- 1 can Pillsbury Grands! Homestyle refrigerated buttermilk biscuits (8 biscuits)
- ½ cup mocha cappuccino–flavored hazelnut spread

1 In deep fryer or 3-quart heavy saucepan, heat oil to 375°F. In shallow bowl or plate, mix sugar and espresso powder; set aside.

2 Separate dough into 8 biscuits; press each into 4-inch round. Spoon 1 tablespoon of the hazelnut spread onto each round. Fold dough over filling; firmly press edges to seal.

3 Gently place 3 biscuits in hot oil. Cook 3 minutes, gently turning once with tongs, until deep golden brown. Drain on paper towels. Roll beignets in sugar mixture. Repeat with remaining biscuits, cooking 2 or 3 at a time. Serve warm.

1 Beignet: Calories 400; Total Fat 24g (Saturated Fat 6g; Trans Fat 0g); Cholesterol 0mg; Sodium 580mg; Total Carbohydrate 42g (Dietary Fiber 0g); Protein 4g **Exchanges:** 1½ Starch, 1½ Other Carbohydrate, 4½ Fat **Carbohydrate Choices:** 3

cherry-almond swirls

prep time: 25 Minutes • **start to finish:** 45 Minutes • 12 rolls

- ¼ cup granulated sugar
- ½ cup slivered almonds
- 3 oz (from 8-oz package) cream cheese, cut into cubes, softened
- ¼ teaspoon vanilla
- ⅛ teaspoon almond extract
- 1 egg yolk
- 1 can Pillsbury refrigerated crescent dinner rolls (8 rolls) or 1 can Pillsbury refrigerated Crescent Dough Sheet
- ¼ cup cherry preserves
- ½ cup powdered sugar
- 2 teaspoons water

1 Heat oven to 375°F. Spray 12 regular-size muffin cups with cooking spray.

2 In food processor, place granulated sugar and almonds. Cover; process about 30 seconds or until almonds are finely ground. Add cream cheese, vanilla, almond extract and egg yolk. Cover; process about 10 seconds or until well blended.

3 If using crescent rolls: Unroll dough into 1 large rectangle on lightly floured surface. With floured rolling pin or fingers, roll or press dough into 12x9-inch rectangle, firmly pressing perforations to seal. If using dough sheet: Unroll dough on lightly floured surface. With floured rolling pin or fingers, roll or press dough into 12x9-inch rectangle.

4 Spread cream cheese mixture evenly over rectangle. Starting with 1 long side, roll up dough into log (filling will be soft). With serrated knife, cut log into 12 slices; place slices, cut side up, in muffin cups.

5 Bake 11 to 15 minutes or until light golden brown. With handle of wooden spoon, make indentation in center of each roll. Spoon 1 teaspoon preserves into each indentation. Bake 2 to 4 minutes longer or until golden brown. Run knife around edge of muffin cups to loosen; remove rolls to cooling racks.

6 In small bowl, mix powdered sugar and water until smooth; drizzle over rolls. Serve warm or at room temperature. Store in refrigerator.

1 Roll: Calories 180; Total Fat 9g (Saturated Fat 3g; Trans Fat 1g); Cholesterol 25mg; Sodium 170mg; Total Carbohydrate 22g (Dietary Fiber 0g); Protein 3g **Exchanges:** 1 Starch, ½ Other Carbohydrate, 1½ Fat **Carbohydrate Choices:** 1½

orange scones with penuche drizzle

prep time: 15 Minutes • **start to finish:** 55 Minutes • 8 scones

Scones

- 1 roll Pillsbury refrigerated sugar cookie dough
- 1 cup all-purpose flour
- ⅓ cup chopped toasted* walnuts, if desired
- 1½ teaspoons grated orange peel
- 3 tablespoons whipping cream
- 1 egg, beaten

Penuche **Drizzle**

- 2 tablespoons packed brown sugar
- 4½ teaspoons half-and-half
- 1 tablespoon butter
- ½ cup powdered sugar
- ¼ teaspoon vanilla

1 Heat oven to 400°F. Let cookie dough stand at room temperature 10 minutes to soften.

2 In medium bowl, break up cookie dough. Stir in flour, walnuts, orange peel, whipping cream and egg with wooden spoon until well blended.

3 Place dough on lightly floured surface; gently roll in flour to coat. Knead lightly 10 times (add additional flour if dough is sticky). Roll or pat dough into 8-inch round. Cut into 8 wedges with sharp knife that has been dipped in flour. Place wedges 2 inches apart on large ungreased cookie sheet.

4 Bake 13 to 17 minutes or until golden brown. Remove from cookie sheet to cooling rack; cool 10 minutes.

5 Meanwhile, in 1-quart saucepan, stir together brown sugar, half-and-half and butter. Cook over medium heat 4 to 5 minutes, stirring frequently, until butter is melted and sugar is dissolved. Cool 10 minutes. Stir in powdered sugar and vanilla. Drizzle over scones. Sprinkle with additional grated orange peel, if desired. Serve warm.

*To toast walnuts, sprinkle in ungreased skillet. Cook over medium heat 5 to 7 minutes, stirring frequently until nuts begin to brown, then stirring constantly until nuts are light brown.

1 Scone: Calories 390; Total Fat 15g (Saturated Fat 6g, Trans Fat 0g); Cholesterol 40mg; Sodium 220mg; Total Carbohydrate 59g (Dietary Fiber 0g); Protein 4g **Exchanges:** 1½ Starch, 2½ Other Carbohydrate, 3 Fat **Carbohydrate Choices:** 4

banana–chocolate chip streusel muffins

prep time: 25 Minutes • **start to finish:** 1 Hour 25 Minutes • 10 muffins

- 1 container Pillsbury Gluten Free refrigerated chocolate chip cookie dough
- 2 teaspoons olive oil
- 4 small bananas
- 1 egg
- 2 tablespoons olive oil
- ¾ cup sweet white sorghum flour
- 1½ teaspoons baking powder
- ⅛ teaspoon salt
- ¼ cup sugar

Easy Success Tip

If you are cooking gluten free, always read labels to make sure each recipe ingredient is gluten free. Products and ingredient sources can change.

1 Heat oven to 350°F. In medium bowl, place ⅓ cup of the cookie dough and 2 teaspoons oil. Cover and refrigerate. Let remaining cookie dough stand at room temperature 10 minutes to soften.

2 Meanwhile, place paper baking cup in each of 10 regular-size muffin cups. In small bowl, mash 1 banana (⅓ cup); set aside. Chop remaining 3 bananas into ¼- to ½-inch pieces (1 cup). Place in medium bowl; set aside.

3 In large bowl, break up softened cookie dough. Beat with electric mixer on low speed 30 seconds. Add mashed banana, egg and 2 tablespoons oil. Beat on low speed 1 minute, scraping bowl as needed. Add ½ cup of the flour, the baking powder and salt. Beat on low speed 30 seconds, scraping bowl as needed. Beat on medium speed 1 minute. Gently stir in chopped banana. Divide batter evenly among muffin cups (cups will be full).

4 Remove cookie dough and oil from refrigerator. Add remaining ¼ cup flour and the sugar. Mix with fork 1 to 2 minutes or until crumbly. Spoon 1 rounded tablespoon crumb mixture onto top of each muffin; press in lightly.

5 Bake 25 to 30 minutes or until toothpick inserted in center comes out clean and tops are golden brown. Cool 10 minutes; remove from pan to cooling rack. Cool 20 minutes. Serve warm or cool. Store covered.

1 Muffin: Calories 300; Total Fat 12g (Saturated Fat 4g; Trans Fat 0g); Cholesterol 35mg; Sodium 260mg; Total Carbohydrate 46g (Dietary Fiber 1g); Protein 2g **Exchanges:** ½ Starch, 2½ Other Carbohydrate, 2½ Fat **Carbohydrate Choices:** 3

Bake-Off® Contest 44, 2010 | **Sherry Roper** | San Diego, CA

maple-bacon breakfast rolls

prep time: 20 Minutes • **start to finish:** 45 Minutes • 12 rolls

- **10 slices precooked bacon**
- **1 can Pillsbury refrigerated Crescent Dough Sheet**
- **3 tablespoons butter, softened**
- **5 tablespoons real or maple-flavored syrup**
- **⅓ cup powdered sugar**

1 Roll: Calories 140; Total Fat 7g (Saturated Fat 3.5g; Trans Fat 0g); Cholesterol 10mg; Sodium 230mg; Total Carbohydrate 17g (Dietary Fiber 0g); Protein 2g **Exchanges:** 1 Starch, 1½ Fat **Carbohydrate Choices:** 1

1 Heat oven to 375°F. Microwave bacon as directed on package until very crisp. Drain on paper towels; set aside to cool.

2 Generously spray large cookie sheet (dark cookie sheet not recommended) with cooking spray, or line with cooking parchment paper. Unroll dough on work surface; starting at center, press dough into 12x8-inch rectangle.

3 In small bowl, mix 2 tablespoons of the butter and 2 tablespoons of the syrup with fork or whisk until smooth and creamy. Spread mixture evenly over dough, covering to edges. Finely chop bacon; reserve 1 tablespoon for garnish. Sprinkle remaining bacon over butter mixture. Starting at short end, roll up dough; pinch edge to seal. Wrap roll in plastic wrap; refrigerate 5 minutes so dough will be easier to cut.

4 Unwrap roll; place seam side down on cutting board. Using serrated knife, cut roll into 12 (about ¾-inch) slices. Place slices, cut side up, on cookie sheet.

5 Bake 8 to 13 minutes or until light golden brown. Place waxed paper under cooling rack. Remove rolls from cookie sheet to cooling rack; cool 5 minutes.

6 In small bowl, mix powdered sugar, remaining 1 tablespoon butter and remaining 3 tablespoons syrup with whisk until smooth. Drizzle icing over rolls. Garnish with reserved bacon.

QUICK | 6-INGREDIENTS OR LESS

ginger-cardamom crescent pastries

prep time: 15 Minutes • **start to finish:** 25 Minutes • 16 pastries

- 2 tablespoons sugar
- ½ teaspoon ground cardamom
- ¼ teaspoon ground ginger
- 1 can Pillsbury refrigerated Crescent Dough Sheet
- 1 tablespoon butter, melted

1 Heat oven to 375°F. In small bowl, mix sugar, cardamom and ginger; set aside.

2 Place dough on cutting board; do not unroll. Using serrated knife, cut dough into ½-inch slices. Place 1 inch apart on large ungreased cookie sheet. Press slices into 2-inch rounds. Brush with melted butter; sprinkle tops with 1 tablespoon of the sugar mixture.

3 Bake 7 to 10 minutes or until edges are golden brown. Sprinkle with remaining sugar mixture. Remove from cookie sheet to serving plate. Serve warm.

1 Pastry: Calories 60; Total Fat 2.5g (Saturated Fat 1g, Trans Fat 0g); Cholesterol 0mg; Sodium 115mg; Total Carbohydrate 8g (Dietary Fiber 0g); Protein 1g **Exchanges:** ½ Starch, ½ Fat **Carbohydrate Choices:** ½

Easy Success Tip

Slice the dough as soon as it is removed from the refrigerator. Cold dough is easier to slice.

strawberry–cream cheese pastries

prep time: 20 Minutes • **start to finish:** 50 Minutes • 8 pastries

- 1 package (8 oz) cream cheese, softened
- ½ cup sugar
- 1 tablespoon whipping cream
- ½ teaspoon ground cinnamon
- ½ teaspoon grated lemon peel
- 1 teaspoon lemon juice
- 8 rolls strawberry chewy fruit snack (from 5-oz box)
- 2 cans Pillsbury refrigerated crescent dinner rolls (8 rolls each)
- 1 tablespoon milk
- 2 tablespoons sugar

1 Heat oven to 375°F. In medium bowl, beat cream cheese and ½ cup sugar with electric mixer on medium speed until smooth. Beat in whipping cream, cinnamon, lemon peel and lemon juice.

2 Remove fruit snacks from wrappers; fold each in half lengthwise. Unroll both cans of dough; separate into 8 rectangles, firmly pressing perforations to seal. Place 1 folded fruit roll lengthwise down center of each dough rectangle.

3 Spoon 2 rounded tablespoons cream cheese mixture onto one half of each fruit snack roll; spread slightly. Fold dough rectangle in half crosswise. Place on ungreased cookie sheet; press edges with fork to seal. Brush tops with milk; sprinkle evenly with 2 tablespoons sugar. With sharp knife, cut 3 diagonal slits in top of each square.

4 Bake 13 to 18 minutes or until golden brown. Cool 10 minutes; remove from cookie sheet. Serve warm.

1 Pastry: Calories 430; Total Fat 21g (Saturated Fat 10g, Trans Fat 0g); Cholesterol 35mg; Sodium 570mg; Total Carbohydrate 53g (Dietary Fiber 0g); Protein 6g **Exchanges:** 2 Starch, 1½ Other Carbohydrate, 4 Fat **Carbohydrate Choices:** 3½

chocolate-raspberry crescent ring

prep time: 40 Minutes • **start to finish:** 40 Minutes • 6 servings

- 1 can Pillsbury refrigerated Crescent Dough Sheet or 1 can Pillsbury refrigerated crescent dinner rolls (8 rolls)
- ½ cup semisweet chocolate chips
- ½ teaspoon vegetable oil
- 1 bag (10 or 12 oz) frozen raspberries
- ¼ cup sugar
- ½ cup water
- 1 tablespoon cornstarch

Easy Success Tips

You can make the sauce up to a day ahead. Refrigerate in a microwavable container, then microwave uncovered on High 1 minute to 1 minute 30 seconds or until warm before pouring over the crescent ring.

Save a step and skip straining the sauce, if you wish. Just spoon the sauce straight from the saucepan over the finished ring.

1 Heat oven to 350°F. Spray large cookie sheet with baking spray with flour or line with parchment.

2 If using dough sheet: Unroll dough on work surface. If using crescent rolls: Unroll dough on work surface; separate into 2 rectangles. Overlap long sides to form 13x7-inch rectangle; firmly press edges and perforations to seal.

3 In small microwavable bowl, microwave chocolate chips and oil uncovered on High 2 minutes, stirring once, until chips are softened and can be stirred smooth. Spread chocolate over dough rectangle. Starting with 1 long side, roll up; pinch edge to seal.

4 With serrated knife, cut roll into 12 slices, wiping knife between cuts. Arrange slices, seam side down, on cookie sheet in 7-inch-diameter circle, leaning each slice against previous one. Tuck last one under first to complete ring.

5 Bake 14 to 18 minutes or until golden brown. Tip cookie sheet and use large, flat spatula to slide ring onto serving plate.

6 Meanwhile, in 4-quart saucepan, mix raspberries, sugar and ¼ cup of the water. Heat to boiling over medium-high heat. Break up berries with wooden spoon if frozen together. Cook 5 minutes, stirring frequently, until berries burst. In small bowl, mix cornstarch and remaining ¼ cup water. Stir into boiling mixture; cook 2 minutes longer or until sauce is very thick. Strain sauce through fine-mesh strainer. Spoon ¼ cup sauce over warm crescent ring. Serve with remaining sauce.

1 Serving: Calories 270; Total Fat 9g (Saturated Fat 4g; Trans Fat 0g); Cholesterol 0mg; Sodium 290mg; Total Carbohydrate 41g (Dietary Fiber 4g); Protein 4g **Exchanges:** 1 Starch, 1½ Other Carbohydrate, 2 Fat **Carbohydrate Choices:** 3

CHAPTER 6

cookies and bars

Bake-Off® Contest 47, 2014 | **Sarah Meuser** | New Milford, CT

hot chocolate–marshmallow cookies

prep time: 20 Minutes • **start to finish:** 55 Minutes • 1 dozen cookies

- 1 roll Pillsbury refrigerated chocolate chip cookie dough
- 1 cup chocolate-flavored hazelnut spread
- 3 tablespoons unsweetened baking cocoa
- ¾ teaspoon chili powder
- ½ teaspoon ground cinnamon
- 6 large marshmallows, cut in half

1 Heat oven to 350°F. Line large cookie sheet with cooking parchment paper. Let cookie dough stand at room temperature 10 minutes to soften.

2 In large bowl, break up cookie dough. Add hazelnut spread, cocoa, chili powder and cinnamon. Beat with electric mixer on low speed about 2 minutes or until well blended.

3 Shape dough into 12 (2-inch) balls. Flatten each ball into 3-inch round. Shape each cookie dough round around marshmallow half, covering completely. Place 2 inches apart on cookie sheet.

4 Bake 10 to 13 minutes or until surface of cookie appears cracked and marshmallow shows through. Cool 5 minutes; remove from cookie sheet to cooling rack. Cool 5 minutes longer. Serve warm. Store in tightly covered container.

1 Cookie: Calories 340; Total Fat 18g (Saturated Fat 6g; Trans Fat 0g); Cholesterol 5mg; Sodium 150mg; Total Carbohydrate 43g (Dietary Fiber 1g); Protein 3g **Exchanges:** 1 Starch, 2 Other Carbohydrate, 3½ Fat **Carbohydrate Choices:** 3

Bake-Off® Contest 47, 2014 | **Christine Southard** | Noble, OK

chocolate–almond butter turtles

prep time: 30 Minutes • **start to finish:** 1 Hour 10 Minutes • 2 dozen cookies

- 1 roll Pillsbury refrigerated sugar cookie dough
- ⅔ cup crunchy almond butter
- ½ teaspoon vanilla
- 1 cup semisweet chocolate chips
- 24 caramels, unwrapped
- 1½ teaspoons water
- 24 milk or dark chocolate-covered almonds

1 Heat oven to 350°F. Let cookie dough stand at room temperature 10 minutes to soften.

2 In large bowl, break up cookie dough. Add almond butter and vanilla. Mix with wooden spoon, or knead with hands, until well blended. Drop dough by rounded tablespoonfuls 2 inches apart onto ungreased cookie sheets.

3 Bake 13 to 18 minutes or until edges are golden brown. Cool 1 minute; remove from cookie sheets to cooling racks. Cool completely, about 10 minutes.

4 In small microwavable bowl, microwave chocolate chips uncovered on High 45 to 60 seconds, stirring once, until chips are softened and can be stirred smooth. Spoon and spread 1 teaspoon chocolate onto each cookie.

5 In another small microwavable bowl, microwave caramels and water uncovered on High 1 minute to 1 minute 30 seconds, stirring once, until mixture can be stirred smooth. Spoon about 1 teaspoon caramel onto center of each cookie; top with almond. Store in tightly covered container.

1 Cookie: Calories 220; Total Fat 11g (Saturated Fat 3g; Trans Fat 0g); Cholesterol 0mg; Sodium 110mg; Total Carbohydrate 27g (Dietary Fiber 1g); Protein 3g **Exchanges:** 1 Starch, 1 Other Carbohydrate, 2 Fat **Carbohydrate Choices:** 2

big birthday cookie

prep time: 10 Minutes • **start to finish:** 1 Hour • 12 wedges

- 1 roll Pillsbury refrigerated chocolate chip cookie dough
- Decorating icing in tubes
- Candy sprinkles

1 Heat oven to 350°F. In ungreased 12-inch pizza pan, break up cookie dough. With floured fingers, press dough evenly in pan.

2 Bake 15 to 20 minutes or until golden brown. Cool completely in pan on cooling rack, about 30 minutes. Decorate as desired with icing and sprinkles. Cut into wedges.

1 Wedge (Undecorated): Calories 320; Total Fat 17g (Saturated Fat 4g; Trans Fat 1g); Cholesterol 5mg; Sodium 200mg; Total Carbohydrate 34g (Dietary Fiber 1g); Protein 7g **Exchanges:** 1 Starch, 1½ Other Carbohydrate, ½ High-Fat Meat, 2½ Fat **Carbohydrate Choices:** 2

Bake-Off® Contest 46, 2013 | **Sue Odren** | Sand Lake, MI

cherry sugar cookie macaroons

prep time: 25 Minutes • **start to finish:** 1 Hour 40 Minutes • 3 dozen cookies

- 1 roll Pillsbury refrigerated sugar cookie dough
- ¾ cup chopped macadamia nuts
- ¾ cup coarsely chopped dried tart cherries
- 1 bag (7 oz) sweetened flaked coconut (about 2½ cups)
- 2 teaspoons vanilla
- 1 cup red tart cherry preserves

1 Heat oven to 350°F. Line cookie sheets with cooking parchment paper. Let cookie dough stand at room temperature 10 minutes to soften.

2 In medium bowl, break up cookie dough. Add nuts, cherries, coconut and vanilla. Mix with wooden spoon, or knead with hands, until well blended. Shape rounded tablespoonfuls of dough into balls. Place 2 inches apart on cookie sheets.

3 Bake 15 to 20 minutes or until edges are light golden brown. Cool 3 minutes. With back of teaspoon, make indentation in center of each cookie. Spoon about 1 teaspoon preserves into each indentation. Cool completely, about 20 minutes. Store in tightly covered container.

1 Cookie: Calories 140; Total Fat 6g (Saturated Fat 2.5g; Trans Fat 0.5g); Cholesterol 0mg; Sodium 60mg; Total Carbohydrate 20g (Dietary Fiber 0g); Protein 1g **Exchanges:** ½ Starch, 1 Other Carbohydrate, 1 Fat **Carbohydrate Choices:** 1

milk-filled cookie cups

prep time: 35 Minutes • **start to finish:** 1 Hour 10 Minutes • 48 cookie cups

- 1 package Pillsbury Ready to Bake!™ refrigerated chocolate chip cookies
- 1 cup semisweet, dark or milk chocolate chips
- 1 cup milk

1 Heat oven to 350°F. Spray 48 mini muffin cups with cooking spray. Cut each cookie in half; press each half into bottom of muffin cup.

2 Bake 8 to 11 minutes or until golden brown. With end of wooden spoon handle, immediately press indentation into each cookie cup. Place 8 chocolate chips into each indentation. Let stand about 2 minutes or until melted.

3 Using back of teaspoon, spread chocolate to completely coat inside of cookie cup to prevent milk from leaking out. (Return muffin pan to oven 30 seconds to 1 minute to melt chips if needed.) Cool 15 minutes; remove cookies from cups to plate. Refrigerate if desired to set chocolate.

4 Store in tightly covered container at room temperature up to 2 days. Fill cookie cups with milk just before serving.

1 Cookie Cup: Calories 60; Total Fat 3g (Saturated Fat 1.5g; Trans Fat 0g); Cholesterol 0mg; Sodium 35mg; Total Carbohydrate 8g (Dietary Fiber 0g); Protein 0g **Exchanges:** ½ Other Carbohydrate, ½ Fat **Carbohydrate Choices:** ½

Easy Success Tips

If you only have one mini muffin pan, refrigerate the rest of the dough while baking and cooling the first batch. Cool the pan completely, then bake the remaining dough, adding 1 to 2 minutes to the bake time.

Substitute peanut butter cookies for chocolate chip, and fill the cookie cups with chocolate milk. Or try sugar cookies, white vanilla baking chips instead of chocolate chips, and fill with strawberry milk.

salted caramel–chocolate chip cookies

prep time: 20 Minutes • **start to finish:** 1 Hour 30 Minutes • 2 dozen cookies

- 1 roll Pillsbury refrigerated chocolate chip cookie dough
- ⅓ cup all-purpose flour
- ½ cup finely chopped pecans
- 24 caramels, unwrapped
- 2 tablespoons half-and-half
- ⅓ cup semisweet chocolate chips, melted
- 1 teaspoon coarse sea salt

1 Heat oven to 350°F. In large bowl, break up cookie dough. Stir or knead in flour until well blended. Shape tablespoonfuls of dough into balls; roll in pecans, pressing into dough. Place 1 inch apart on ungreased cookie sheets.

2 Bake 12 to 16 minutes or until edges are light golden brown. With handle of wooden spoon, make indentation in center of each cookie. Cool 1 minute; remove from cookie sheets to cooling racks. Cool completely, about 20 minutes.

3 In microwavable bowl, microwave caramels and half-and-half uncovered on High 1 to 2 minutes, stirring once, until caramels are melted. Spoon about 1 teaspoon caramel into indentation of each cookie. Cool 15 minutes.

4 Drizzle with melted chocolate; sprinkle with salt. Let stand about 15 minutes or until chocolate is set.

1 Cookie: Calories 170; Total Fat 8g (Saturated Fat 2.5g; Trans Fat 1g); Cholesterol 0mg; Sodium 190mg; Total Carbohydrate 23g (Dietary Fiber 0g); Protein 1g **Exchanges:** ½ Starch, 1 Other Carbohydrate, 1½ Fat **Carbohydrate Choices:** 1½

chocolate chip–toasted pecan cookies

prep time: 15 Minutes • **start to finish:** 40 Minutes • 2 dozen cookies

- 1 container Pillsbury Gluten Free refrigerated chocolate chip cookie dough
- ½ cup chopped pecans, toasted*
- ¼ teaspoon coarse sea salt
- ¾ cup powdered sugar

1 Heat oven to 350°F. In medium bowl, break up cookie dough. Add pecans and salt; mix with wooden spoon, or knead with hands, until well blended.

2 Shape dough into 24 (1¼-inch) balls. Place 2 inches apart on ungreased cookie sheets.

3 Bake 11 to 13 minutes or until edges are golden brown. Cool 2 minutes; remove from cookie sheets to cooling racks. Cool 3 minutes.

4 In small bowl, place powdered sugar; roll cookies in powdered sugar to coat. Let stand 5 minutes. Roll in powdered sugar again. Store loosely covered.

*To toast pecans, heat oven to 350°F. Spread nuts in an ungreased shallow pan. Bake uncovered 6 to 10 minutes, stirring occasionally, until light brown.

1 Cookie: Calories 100; Total Fat 5g (Saturated Fat 1.5g, Trans Fat 0g); Cholesterol 5mg; Sodium 90mg; Total Carbohydrate 14g (Dietary Fiber 0g); Protein 0g **Exchanges:** 1 Other Carbohydrate, 1 Fat **Carbohydrate Choices:** 1

Easy Success Tip

If you are cooking gluten free, always read labels to make sure each recipe ingredient is gluten free. Products and ingredient sources can change.

candied bacon–peanut butter cookies

prep time: 40 Minutes • **start to finish:** 2 Hours 10 Minutes • 2½ dozen cookies

Cookies

- 20 slices center-cut bacon
- 2 tablespoons packed brown sugar
- 1 roll Pillsbury refrigerated peanut butter cookie dough

Filling

- ½ cup butter
- ½ cup creamy peanut butter
- 2 teaspoons vanilla
- 1½ cups powdered sugar
- ⅓ cup dark chocolate chips

1 Cookie: Calories 170; Total Fat 9g (Saturated Fat 4g, Trans Fat 0g); Cholesterol 10mg; Sodium 160mg; Total Carbohydrate 18g (Dietary Fiber 0g); Protein 2g **Exchanges:** 1 Other Carbohydrate, 2 Fat **Carbohydrate Choices:** 1

Easy Success Tips

We recommend center-cut bacon for this recipe because it fits perfectly crosswise in the pan.

Sprinkle tops of cookies with coarse sea salt for a sweet and salty peanut butter cookie.

1 Heat oven to 400°F. Line 15x10x1-inch pan with cooking parchment paper. Arrange bacon slices, sides touching, in pan; sprinkle with brown sugar. Bake 15 to 20 minutes or until crisp. Remove bacon from pan to plate or cutting board. Cool 15 minutes; coarsely chop.

2 Reduce oven temperature to 350°F. In medium bowl, break up cookie dough. Stir in ½ cup of the bacon (reserve remaining bacon for topping). Shape dough into 30 (1¼-inch) balls. Place 1½ inches apart on ungreased cookie sheets.

3 Bake 10 to 15 minutes or until edges are golden brown. Immediately press back of teaspoon in center of each cookie to make indentation. Cool 5 minutes; remove from cookie sheets to cooling racks. Cool completely, about 15 minutes.

4 Meanwhile, in 2-quart saucepan, heat butter and peanut butter over medium heat, stirring occasionally, until melted. Remove from heat; stir in vanilla. Cool 1 minute. Add powdered sugar; beat with electric mixer on low speed until smooth. Pipe or spoon filling into center of each cookie. Sprinkle with reserved bacon, pressing lightly into filling.

5 In small microwavable bowl, microwave chocolate chips uncovered on High 30 to 60 seconds, stirring once, until chips are softened and can be stirred smooth. Spoon melted chocolate into small resealable food-storage plastic bag. Cut off tiny corner of bag; squeeze bag to drizzle chocolate over cookies. Let stand 15 minutes or until chocolate is set. Store in refrigerator.

Bake-Off® Contest 43, 2008 | **Karry Edwards** | Sandy, UT

jumbo honey-roasted peanut butter sandwich cookies

prep time: 25 Minutes • **start to finish:** 1 Hour 10 Minutes • 8 sandwich cookies

- 2 packages (8 oz each) cream cheese, softened
- ½ cup creamy peanut butter
- 2 tablespoons honey
- 1 cup powdered sugar
- 1 roll Pillsbury refrigerated peanut butter cookie dough
- ¾ to 1 cup honey-roasted peanuts, coarsely chopped

1 In large bowl, beat cream cheese, peanut butter and honey with electric mixer on medium speed until smooth. Add powdered sugar; beat just until smooth. Cover; refrigerate at least 1 hour.

2 Heat oven to 350°F. Bake cookies as directed on package. Cool completely.

3 For each sandwich cookie, spread ⅓ cup cream cheese filling on bottom of 1 cookie. Top with second cookie, bottom side down; gently press together. Roll edge of filling in chopped peanuts. Serve immediately, or store in single layer tightly covered in refrigerator up to 4 hours (cookies stored longer become very soft).

1 Sandwich Cookie: Calories 730; Total Fat 47g (Saturated Fat 18g; Trans Fat 2.5g); Cholesterol 70mg; Sodium 560mg; Total Carbohydrate 60g (Dietary Fiber 2g); Protein 16g **Exchanges:** 1 Starch, 3 Other Carbohydrate, 2 High-Fat Meat, 6 Fat **Carbohydrate Choices:** 4

marshmallow-lemon snowdrifts

prep time: 25 Minutes • **start to finish:** 1 Hour • 2 dozen cookies

- 1 roll Pillsbury refrigerated sugar cookie dough
- ⅓ cup all-purpose flour
- 1 teaspoon grated lemon peel
- ⅓ cup coarse sugar
- 1 jar (7 oz) marshmallow creme (1½ cups)
- 1 cup butter, softened
- ½ teaspoon vanilla
- 2½ cups powdered sugar
- ½ cup plus 2 teaspoons lemon curd

1 Heat oven to 350°F. In large bowl, break up cookie dough. Stir or knead in flour and lemon peel until well blended. Shape dough into 24 (1¼-inch) balls. Roll balls in coarse sugar to coat completely. Place 2 inches apart on ungreased cookie sheets.

2 Bake 10 to 12 minutes or until edges are golden brown. Cool 1 minute; remove from cookie sheets to cooling racks. Cool completely.

3 In large bowl, beat marshmallow creme, butter and vanilla with electric mixer on medium speed until blended. Beat in powdered sugar until fluffy. Spoon frosting into decorating bag fitted with tip.

4 Spoon a dollop of lemon curd in center of each cookie. Pipe frosting around and on top of lemon curd.

1 Cookie: Calories 260; Total Fat 12g (Saturated Fat 6g; Trans Fat 1.5g); Cholesterol 25mg; Sodium 140mg; Total Carbohydrate 38g (Dietary Fiber 0g); Protein 1g **Exchanges:** ½ Starch, 2 Other Carbohydrate, 2½ Fat **Carbohydrate Choices:** 2½

Easy Success Tip

To make raspberry-flavored cookies, use raspberry preserves instead of the lemon curd and omit the lemon peel from the dough.

caramel apple cookies

prep time: 20 Minutes • **start to finish:** 1 Hour • 2 dozen cookies

- **1 roll Pillsbury refrigerated sugar cookie dough**
- **¼ cup all-purpose flour**
- **¾ cup chopped peeled apple (1 medium)**
- **½ teaspoon apple pie spice**
- **24 caramels, unwrapped**
- **2 tablespoons half-and-half**
- **3 tablespoons chopped pecans**

1 Heat oven to 350°F. In large bowl, break up cookie dough. Stir or knead in flour, apple and apple pie spice until well blended. Drop by rounded tablespoonfuls onto ungreased cookie sheets.

2 Bake 14 to 16 minutes or until edges are golden brown. Cool 1 minute; remove from cookie sheets to cooling racks. Cool completely, about 20 minutes.

3 In small microwavable bowl, microwave caramels and half-and-half uncovered on High 30 to 60 seconds, stirring once, until caramels are melted and mixture can be stirred smooth. Drizzle over tops of cookies; sprinkle with pecans. Store covered in refrigerator.

1 Cookie: Calories 140; Total Fat 5g (Saturated Fat 1.5g; Trans Fat 1g); Cholesterol 0mg; Sodium 90mg; Total Carbohydrate 21g (Dietary Fiber 0g); Protein 1g **Exchanges:** ½ Starch, 1 Other Carbohydrate, 1 Fat **Carbohydrate Choices:** 1½

Bake-Off® Contest 44, 2010 | **Anita Van Gundy** | Des Moines, IA

coconut-filled chocolate delights

prep time: 30 Minutes • **start to finish:** 1 Hour 40 Minutes • 20 cookies

- ¾ cup salted roasted whole almonds
- 1½ cups coconut
- ½ cup sweetened condensed milk (not evaporated)
- 1 package Pillsbury Ready to Bake! refrigerated sugar cookies
- ⅓ cup unsweetened baking cocoa
- ⅓ cup milk chocolate chips

1 Set aside 20 almonds. Chop remaining almonds. In medium bowl, stir chopped almonds, coconut and condensed milk until well blended. Refrigerate 25 minutes for easier handling. Let cookie dough stand at room temperature 10 minutes to soften.

2 Heat oven to 350°F. In large bowl, stir or knead cookie dough and cocoa until well blended. For each cookie, press 1 rounded tablespoon dough into 3-inch round. Place 1 tablespoon coconut mixture on center of each round. Wrap dough around filling, pressing edges to seal; shape into a ball.

3 Place balls 3 inches apart on ungreased cookie sheets. Press each ball with fingers into 2½-inch round. Press 1 whole almond on each cookie.

4 Bake 9 to 12 minutes or until puffed and edges are set. Immediately remove from cookie sheets to cooling racks. Cool completely, about 30 minutes.

5 In small microwavable bowl, microwave chocolate chips uncovered on High 10 to 20 seconds, stirring every 10 seconds, until chips are softened and can be stirred smooth. Drizzle chocolate over cookies; let stand until set. Store in tightly covered container.

1 Cookie: Calories 180; Total Fat 10g (Saturated Fat 4g; Trans Fat 0g); Cholesterol 0mg; Sodium 85mg; Total Carbohydrate 21g (Dietary Fiber 1g); Protein 2g **Exchanges:** ½ Starch, 1 Other Carbohydrate, 2 Fat **Carbohydrate Choices:** 1½

five-ingredient pumpkin cookies

prep time: 15 Minutes • **start to finish:** 1 Hour 10 Minutes • 1½ dozen cookies

- 1 roll Pillsbury refrigerated sugar cookie dough
- 2 tablespoons pumpkin pie spice
- ½ cup canned pumpkin (not pumpkin pie mix)
- 1 package (8 oz) cream cheese
- 1 cup powdered sugar

Easy Success Tip

In a pinch, canned cream cheese frosting can be used instead of the cream cheese and powdered sugar mixture.

1 Heat oven to 350°F. In large bowl, break up cookie dough. Add pumpkin pie spice and pumpkin. Beat with electric mixer on medium speed until well blended.

2 Drop dough by rounded tablespoonfuls about 2 inches apart onto ungreased cookie sheet.

3 Bake 14 to 16 minutes. Cool 5 minutes; remove from cookie sheet to cooling rack. Cool completely, about 30 minutes.

4 Place unwrapped cream cheese in medium microwavable bowl. Microwave uncovered on High 1 to 2 minutes, stirring every 30 seconds, until softened. Stir in powdered sugar until smooth. Spread over cookies.

1 Cookie: Calories 180; Total Fat 9g (Saturated Fat 4g; Trans Fat 1.5g); Cholesterol 15mg; Sodium 125mg; Total Carbohydrate 24g (Dietary Fiber 0g); Protein 1g **Exchanges:** 1 Starch, ½ Other Carbohydrate, 1½ Fat **Carbohydrate Choices:** 1½

chewy gingersnaps with white chocolate drizzle

prep time: 25 Minutes • **start to finish:** 1 Hour 25 Minutes • 2½ dozen cookies

- 1 container Pillsbury Gluten Free refrigerated pie and pastry dough
- 1 cup sugar
- 1 tablespoon ground ginger
- 1 teaspoon ground cinnamon
- 1 teaspoon baking soda
- ¼ cup molasses
- 1 cup white vanilla baking chips

1 Cookie: Calories 200; Total Fat 11g (Saturated Fat 4.5g; Trans Fat 0g); Cholesterol 0mg; Sodium 240mg; Total Carbohydrate 25g (Dietary Fiber 0g); Protein 0g **Exchanges:** 1½ Other Carbohydrate, 2 Fat **Carbohydrate Choices:** 1½

1 Heat oven to 350°F. Let cookie dough stand at room temperature 10 minutes to soften.

2 In large bowl, break up cookie dough. Add all remaining ingredients except baking chips. Beat with electric mixer on medium-low speed about 2 minutes or until well blended.

3 Shape dough into 30 (1½-inch) balls. Place 3 inches apart on ungreased cookie sheets (dark cookie sheets not recommended); flatten with fingers into 2-inch rounds.

4 Bake 10 to 14 minutes or until edges are set. Cool 4 minutes; remove from cookie sheets to cooling racks. Cool completely, about 15 minutes.

5 In small microwavable bowl, microwave baking chips uncovered on High 45 to 60 seconds, stirring once, until chips are softened and can be stirred smooth. Drizzle over cookies. Store covered.

Easy Success Tip

If you are cooking gluten free, always read labels to make sure each recipe ingredient is gluten free. Products and ingredient sources can change.

fudgy chocolate chip–toffee bars

prep time: 25 Minutes • **start to finish:** 3 Hours 15 Minutes • 32 bars

- ½ cup butter, melted
- 2 cups graham cracker crumbs (32 squares)
- 1 bag (8 oz) toffee bits
- 1 roll Pillsbury refrigerated chocolate chip cookie dough
- 2 cups semisweet chocolate chips (about 12 oz)
- 1 can (14 oz) sweetened condensed milk (not evaporated)
- 1 tablespoon butter
- 1 teaspoon vanilla

Easy Success Tip

To crush graham crackers, place in large resealable food-storage plastic bag; crush with rolling pan or meat mallet. Or, save prep time by purchasing graham cracker crumbs—look for them in boxes in the baking aisle of the grocery store.

1 Heat oven to 350°F (325°F for dark or nonstick pan). Spray bottom only of 13x9-inch pan with cooking spray.

2 In medium bowl, stir together ½ cup butter, 1½ cups of the cracker crumbs and ¾ cup of the toffee bits. Press mixture evenly in bottom of pan. Refrigerate about 15 minutes or until firm.

3 Meanwhile, let cookie dough stand at room temperature 10 minutes to soften. In 2-quart saucepan, heat chocolate chips, condensed milk and 1 tablespoon butter over medium heat, stirring frequently, until chips are melted and mixture is smooth. Remove from heat; stir in vanilla. Spread mixture over crust.

4 In medium bowl, break up cookie dough. Mix in remaining ½ cup cracker crumbs with wooden spoon until well blended. Crumble mixture over chocolate layer. Sprinkle with remaining ¾ cup toffee bits.

5 Bake 25 to 35 minutes or until golden brown. Cool completely in pan on cooling rack, about 2 hours. For a firmer bar, refrigerate 30 minutes. Cut into 8 rows by 4 rows.

1 Bar: Calories 270; Total Fat 14g (Saturated Fat 7g; Trans Fat 1g); Cholesterol 15mg; Sodium 130mg; Total Carbohydrate 32g (Dietary Fiber 1g); Protein 2g **Exchanges:** ½ Starch, 1½ Other Carbohydrate, 3 Fat **Carbohydrate Choices:** 2

chewy oatmeal-raisin breakfast bars

prep time: 15 Minutes • **start to finish:** 1 Hour 40 Minutes • 18 bars

- 1 package Pillsbury Big Deluxe™ refrigerated oatmeal raisin cookies
- 1 cup old-fashioned oats
- ½ cup coarsely chopped walnuts
- ½ cup flaked coconut
- ½ cup miniature semisweet chocolate chips
- ½ cup sweetened dried cranberries
- ¼ cup mocha cappuccino-flavored hazelnut spread

1 Heat oven 350°F. Line 9-inch square pan with foil, extending foil 1 inch over 2 opposite sides of pan. Let cookie dough stand at room temperature 10 minutes to soften.

2 In large bowl, break up cookie dough. Add oats, walnuts, coconut, chocolate chips and cranberries. Mix with wooden spoon, or knead with hands, until well blended. Press mixture firmly in pan.

3 Bake 20 to 30 minutes or until golden brown. Cool 15 minutes. Refrigerate 30 minutes. Remove bars from pan using edges of foil as handles. Cut into 6 rows by 3 rows.

4 In small microwavable bowl, microwave hazelnut spread uncovered on High 30 to 35 seconds or until melted. Drizzle over bars.

1 Bar: Calories 220; Total Fat 10g (Saturated Fat 3.5g; Trans Fat 0g); Cholesterol 0mg; Sodium 80mg; Total Carbohydrate 29g (Dietary Fiber 2g); Protein 2g **Exchanges:** ½ Starch, 1½ Other Carbohydrate, 2 Fat **Carbohydrate Choices:** 2

chewy fruit and nut bars

prep time: 15 Minutes • **start to finish:** 1 Hour 55 Minutes • 16 bars

- 1 package Pillsbury Big Deluxe refrigerated oatmeal raisin cookies
- 1 cup old-fashioned oats
- ½ cup coarsely chopped toasted* pecans
- ½ cup chopped dates
- ½ cup golden raisins or dried cherries
- ⅓ cup miniature semisweet chocolate chips
- 1 tablespoon real maple syrup
- ¼ teaspoon ground nutmeg

1 Heat oven to 350°F. Line 9-inch square pan with foil, extending foil 1 inch over 2 opposite sides of pan. Let cookie dough stand at room temperature 10 minutes to soften.

2 In large bowl, break up cookie dough. Add remaining ingredients; mix with wooden spoon, or knead with hands, until well blended. Press firmly in pan with fingers.

3 Bake 25 to 30 minutes or until golden brown. Cool completely in pan on cooling rack, about 1 hour. Cut into 4 rows by 4 rows.

*To toast pecans, heat oven to 350°F. Spread nuts in an ungreased shallow pan. Bake uncovered 6 to 10 minutes, stirring occasionally, until light brown.

1 Bar: Calories 210; Total Fat 8g (Saturated Fat 2.5g, Trans Fat 0g); Cholesterol 0mg; Sodium 75mg; Total Carbohydrate 32g (Dietary Fiber 2g); Protein 2g **Exchanges:** ½ Starch, 1½ Other Carbohydrate, 1½ Fat **Carbohydrate Choices:** 2

peanut butter and jelly bars

prep time: 10 Minutes • **start to finish:** 1 Hour • 24 bars

- 1 roll Pillsbury refrigerated peanut butter cookie dough
- ½ cup peanut butter chips
- ¼ cup creamy peanut butter
- 1 container (1 lb) vanilla creamy ready-to-spread frosting
- ¼ cup seedless raspberry jam or strawberry jelly

Easy Success Tips

Use any flavor jam or jelly you like in these easy bars.

For chocolate-flavored bars, substitute semisweet chocolate chips for the peanut butter chips and chocolate frosting for the vanilla frosting.

1 Heat oven to 350°F (325°F for dark or nonstick pan). Spray 13x9-inch pan with cooking spray. Break up cookie dough in pan; press evenly in pan. Press peanut butter chips into dough.

2 Bake 15 to 20 minutes or until golden brown. Cool completely in pan on cooling rack, about 30 minutes.

3 In medium bowl, stir peanut butter until smooth. Stir in frosting until well blended. Spread over bars.

4 In small bowl, stir jam until smooth. Drop jam by teaspoonfuls over frosting. With tip of knife, swirl jam for marbled design. Cut into 6 rows by 4 rows.

1 Bar: Calories 200; Total Fat 9g (Saturated Fat 2g; Trans Fat 2g); Cholesterol 0mg; Sodium 150mg; Total Carbohydrate 28g (Dietary Fiber 0g); Protein 2g **Exchanges:** 1 Starch, 1 Other Carbohydrate, 1½ Fat **Carbohydrate Choices:** 2

chewy chocolate chip–almond bars

prep time: 15 Minutes • **start to finish:** 2 Hours 25 Minutes • 12 bars

- 1 package Pillsbury Ready to Bake! refrigerated chocolate chip cookies
- 2 oz marzipan, diced (¼ cup)
- ¼ teaspoon almond extract
- 1 can (14 oz) sweetened condensed milk (not evaporated)
- ½ cup crunchy almond butter
- ½ cup semisweet chocolate chips
- ½ cup sliced almonds

1 Bar: Calories 430; Total Fat 21g (Saturated Fat 7g; Trans Fat 0g); Cholesterol 10mg; Sodium 190mg; Total Carbohydrate 52g (Dietary Fiber 2g); Protein 7g **Exchanges:** 2½ Starch, 1 Other Carbohydrate, 4 Fat **Carbohydrate Choices:** 3½

1 Heat oven to 350°F. Spray 9-inch square pan with cooking spray.

2 In large bowl, break up cookie dough. Add marzipan and almond extract. Beat with electric mixer on high speed about 2 minutes or until well blended. Press dough evenly in bottom of pan.

3 In small bowl, mix condensed milk and almond butter until smooth; pour over dough. Sprinkle with chocolate chips and almonds.

4 Bake 35 to 40 minutes or until edges are golden brown and center still jiggles slightly. Cool completely in pan on cooling rack, about 1 hour 30 minutes. Cut into 4 rows by 3 rows. Store covered in refrigerator.

ooey-gooey turtle bars

prep time: 20 Minutes • **start to finish:** 4 Hours 25 Minutes • 24 bars

- **1 roll Pillsbury refrigerated sugar cookie dough**
- **2 cups semisweet chocolate chips (about 12 oz)**
- **3 cups chopped pecans**
- **½ cup butter**
- **½ cup packed light brown sugar**
- **1 jar (12.25 oz) caramel topping**
- **1 cup graham cracker crumbs (16 squares)**

1 Heat oven to 350°F (325°F for dark or nonstick pan). Press cookie dough evenly in bottom of ungreased 13x9-inch pan. Sprinkle 1 cup of the chocolate chips and 1½ cups of the pecans over dough; lightly press into dough.

2 In 2-quart saucepan, melt butter over medium-high heat. Stir in brown sugar, caramel topping and graham cracker crumbs. Heat to boiling, stirring constantly. Pour and spread over crust. Sprinkle with remaining 1 cup chocolate chips and 1½ cups pecans.

3 Bake 25 to 32 minutes or until edges are deep golden brown and pecans are lightly toasted. Cool on cooling rack 30 minutes; loosen sides from pan, but do not cut. Cool completely, about 3 hours. For a firmer bar, let stand an additional 2 hours. Cut into 6 rows by 4 rows.

1 Bar: Calories 370; Total Fat 22g (Saturated Fat 7g; Trans Fat 1.5g); Cholesterol 15mg; Sodium 160mg; Total Carbohydrate 40g (Dietary Fiber 2g); Protein 3g **Exchanges:** 1 Starch, 1½ Other Carbohydrate, 4½ Fat **Carbohydrate Choices:** 2½

caramel chai bars

prep time: 15 Minutes • **start to finish:** 2 Hours 35 Minutes • 16 bars

- 1 roll Pillsbury refrigerated sugar cookie dough
- 1 package (1.1 oz) chai tea latte mix (from 8.8-oz box)
- ½ cup caramel-flavored sundae syrup
- 2 tablespoons all-purpose flour
- ½ cup ground walnuts

1 Heat oven to 350°F. In large bowl, knead cookie dough and dry tea mix until well blended.

2 Break up three-fourths of the dough in ungreased 8-inch square pan; press evenly in bottom of pan. (If dough is sticky, use floured fingers.) Bake 12 to 17 minutes or until light golden brown.

3 Meanwhile, in small bowl, mix caramel syrup and flour. In another small bowl, knead remaining one-fourth of the dough and the walnuts. Gently drizzle caramel mixture over partially baked crust. Crumble walnut dough over caramel.

4 Bake 22 to 29 minutes longer or until top is golden brown and firm to the touch and caramel is bubbly. Cool completely in pan on cooling rack, about 1 hour 30 minutes. Cut into 4 rows by 4 rows.

1 Bar: Calories 190; Total Fat 9g (Saturated Fat 1.5g; Trans Fat 1.5g); Cholesterol 10mg; Sodium 140mg; Total Carbohydrate 27g (Dietary Fiber 0g); Protein 2g **Exchanges:** ½ Starch, 1½ Other Carbohydrate, 1½ Fat **Carbohydrate Choices:** 2

choco-cherry cheesecake bars

prep time: 30 Minutes • **start to finish:** 2 Hours 25 Minutes • 48 bars

- 1 roll Pillsbury refrigerated sugar cookie dough
- 1 egg, separated
- 1 package (8 oz) cream cheese, softened
- 2 whole eggs
- 1 can (14 oz) sweetened condensed milk (not evaporated)
- ¼ teaspoon almond extract
- 3 drops red food color
- 1 jar (10 oz) maraschino cherries, finely chopped, drained on paper towels
- 2 cups semisweet chocolate chips (about 12 oz)
- ½ cup butter, cut into pieces
- ½ cup whipping cream

1 Heat oven to 350°F. Break up cookie dough in ungreased 15x10x1-inch pan; with floured fingers, press dough evenly in bottom of pan. Bake 10 to 15 minutes or until light golden brown.

2 In small bowl, beat 1 egg white until frothy. Brush egg white over partially baked crust. Bake 3 minutes longer or until egg white is set.

3 In large bowl, beat cream cheese with electric mixer on medium speed until smooth. Add egg yolk, 2 eggs, the condensed milk, almond extract and food color; beat until well blended. Stir in chopped cherries. Pour over crust.

4 Bake 16 to 20 minutes longer or until set. Cool completely in pan on cooling rack, about 45 minutes.

5 Meanwhile, in 2-quart saucepan, heat chocolate chips and butter over low heat, stirring frequently, until melted and smooth. Remove from heat; cool 20 minutes. Stir in whipping cream until well blended. Spread over bars. Refrigerate about 30 minutes or until chocolate is set. Cut into 8 rows by 6 rows. Store in refrigerator.

1 Bar: Calories 160; Total Fat 9g (Saturated Fat 5g, Trans Fat 0.5g); Cholesterol 25mg; Sodium 80mg; Total Carbohydrate 17g (Dietary Fiber 0g); Protein 2g **Exchanges:** 1 Starch, 1 ½ Fat **Carbohydrate Choices:** 1

red velvet bars

prep time: 20 Minutes • **start to finish:** 2 Hours • 24 bars

Bars

- 2 rolls Pillsbury refrigerated sugar cookie dough
- ⅓ cup unsweetened baking cocoa
- 1 bottle (1 oz) red food color
- 1 egg

Frosting

- ¼ cup all-purpose flour
- ¾ cup milk
- ¾ cup sugar
- ¾ cup butter, softened
- 1½ teaspoons vanilla

1 Heat oven to 350°F. Let cookie dough stand at room temperature 10 minutes to soften.

2 In large bowl, break up cookie dough. Add cocoa, food color and egg. Beat with electric mixer on medium speed 1 minute, scraping bowl frequently. Spread in bottom of ungreased 13x9-inch pan.

3 Bake 25 to 30 minutes or until center is set. Cool completely in pan on cooling rack, about 1 hour.

4 In 1-quart saucepan, mix flour and milk with whisk until smooth. Cook over medium heat 3 to 5 minutes, stirring constantly, until mixture is very thick. Remove from heat; cool 10 minutes.

5 In large bowl, beat sugar and butter with electric mixer on medium speed 1 minute or until light and fluffy. Gradually add flour mixture by tablespoonfuls, beating on high speed until smooth. Beat in vanilla. Frost bars. Cut into 6 rows by 4 rows.

1 Bar: Calories 180; Total Fat 10g (Saturated Fat 5g, Trans Fat 0g); Cholesterol 25mg; Sodium 120mg; Total Carbohydrate 20g (Dietary Fiber 0g); Protein 1g **Exchanges:** ½ Starch, 1 Other Carbohydrate, 2 Fat

easy double-chocolate brownies

prep time: 10 Minutes • **start to finish:** 1 Hour 20 Minutes • 24 brownies

- 1 container Pillsbury Gluten Free refrigerated chocolate chip cookie dough
- 1 cup canned pumpkin (not pumpkin pie mix)
- 1 teaspoon vanilla
- 2 eggs
- ¼ cup unsweetened baking cocoa
- 1 tablespoon packed brown sugar
- 1 teaspoon ground cinnamon

1 Heat oven to 350°F. Let cookie dough stand at room temperature 10 minutes to soften. Spray 13x9-inch pan with cooking spray.

2 In large bowl, break up cookie dough. Add remaining ingredients; beat with electric mixer on medium speed about 2 minutes or until well blended. Spread evenly in pan.

3 Bake 22 to 30 minutes or until toothpick inserted in center comes out clean. Cool completely in pan on cooling rack, about 30 minutes. Cut into 6 rows by 4 rows. Store loosely covered.

1 Brownie: Calories 90; Total Fat 4g (Saturated Fat 1.5g; Trans Fat 0g); Cholesterol 20mg; Sodium 70mg; Total Carbohydrate 12g (Dietary Fiber 0g); Protein 1g **Exchanges:** 1 Starch, ½ Fat **Carbohydrate Choices:** 1

Easy Success Tip

If you are cooking gluten free, always read labels to make sure each recipe ingredient is gluten free. Products and ingredient sources can change.

chocolate chip–espresso almond bars

prep time: 15 Minutes • **start to finish:** 1 Hour 15 Minutes • 24 bars

- 1 container Pillsbury Gluten Free refrigerated chocolate chip cookie dough
- ½ cup sliced almonds
- 1 tablespoon instant espresso coffee powder or granules
- ½ teaspoon almond extract
- 1 cup powdered sugar
- 1 to 2 tablespoons milk
- ½ teaspoon vanilla

1 Heat oven to 350°F. Spray 13x9-inch pan with cooking spray.

2 In medium bowl, break up cookie dough. Add ¼ cup of the almonds, the coffee powder and almond extract. Mix with wooden spoon, or knead with hands, until well blended. Press dough evenly in bottom of pan.

3 Bake 13 to 18 minutes or until golden brown and center is set. Cool completely in pan on cooling rack, about 30 minutes.

4 In medium bowl, stir powdered sugar, 1 tablespoon of the milk and the vanilla until smooth; add additional milk, 1 teaspoon at a time, until desired spreading consistency. Spread glaze over bars; sprinkle with remaining ¼ cup almonds. Refrigerate about 10 minutes or until glaze is set. Cut into 6 rows by 4 rows.

1 Bar: Calories 100; Total Fat 4.5g (Saturated Fat 1.5g; Trans Fat 0g); Cholesterol 5mg; Sodium 65mg; Total Carbohydrate 16g (Dietary Fiber 0g); Protein 0g **Exchanges:** 1 Other Carbohydrate, 1 Fat **Carbohydrate Choices:** 1

Easy Success Tip

If you are cooking gluten free, always read labels to make sure each recipe ingredient is gluten free. Products and ingredient sources can change.

Metric Conversion Guide

VOLUME

U.S. Units	Canadian Metric	Australian Metric
¼ teaspoon	1 mL	1 ml
½ teaspoon	2 mL	2 ml
1 teaspoon	5 mL	5 ml
1 tablespoon	15 mL	20 ml
¼ cup	50 mL	60 ml
⅓ cup	75 mL	80 ml
½ cup	125 mL	125 ml
⅔ cup	150 mL	170 ml
¾ cup	175 mL	190 ml
1 cup	250 mL	250 ml
1 quart	1 liter	1 liter
1½ quarts	1.5 liters	1.5 liters
2 quarts	2 liters	2 liters
2½ quarts	2.5 liters	2.5 liters
3 quarts	3 liters	3 liters
4 quarts	4 liters	4 liters

WEIGHT

U.S. Units	Canadian Metric	Australian Metric
1 ounce	30 grams	30 grams
2 ounces	55 grams	60 grams
3 ounces	85 grams	90 grams
4 ounces (¼ pound)	115 grams	125 grams
8 ounces (½ pound)	225 grams	225 grams
16 ounces (1 pound)	455 grams	500 grams
1 pound	455 grams	0.5 kilogram

Note: The recipes in this cookbook have not been developed or tested using metric measures. When converting recipes to metric, some variations in quality may be noted.

MEASUREMENTS

Inches	Centimeters
1	2.5
2	5.0
3	7.5
4	10.0
5	12.5
6	15.0
7	17.5
8	20.5
9	23.0
10	25.5
11	28.0
12	30.5
13	33.0

TEMPERATURES

Fahrenheit	Celsius
32°	0°
212°	100°
250°	120°
275°	140°
300°	150°
325°	160°
350°	180°
375°	190°
400°	200°
425°	220°
450°	230°
475°	240°
500°	260°

index

Page numbers in *italics* indicate illustrations
* indicate 6-ingredient-or-less recipes
# indicate quick recipes

A

B

Recipe Testing and Calculating Nutrition Information

Recipe Testing:

- Large eggs and 2% milk were used unless otherwise indicated.
- Fat-free, low-fat, low-sodium or lite products were not used unless indicated.
- No nonstick cookware or bakeware were used unless otherwise indicated. No dark-colored, black or insulated bakeware was used.
- When a pan is specified, a metal pan was used; a baking dish or pie plate means ovenproof glass was used.
- An electric hand mixer was used for mixing only when mixer speeds are specified.

Calculating Nutrition:

- The first ingredient was used wherever a choice is given, such as ⅓ cup sour cream or plain yogurt.
- The first amount was used wherever a range is given, such as 3- to 3½-pound whole chicken.
- The first serving number was used wherever a range is given, such as 4 to 6 servings.
- "If desired" ingredients were not included.
- Only the amount of a marinade or frying oil that is absorbed was included.

C

D

E

F

G

H

I

J

K

L

M

N

O

P

Q

R

S

T

V

W

Z